To my wonderful
Marie R. at the Vill
Pines.

Best wishes
Mazal Tov

Nathan Rosenfeld

M000080531

A SOLDIER
OF CHANCE

A True Story of Resistance,
Endurance And Survival

NATHAN ROSENFELD, Ph.D.

the Peppertree Press
Sarasota, Florida

For information regarding permission,
call 941-922-2662 or contact us at our website:
www.peppertreepublishing.com or write to:
the Peppertree Press, LLC.
Attention: Publisher
1269 First Street, Suite 7
Sarasota, Florida 34236

ISBN: 978-1-61493-038-9

Library of Congress Number: 2012931572

Printed in the U.S.A.

Printed April 2012

Dedicated to the memory of my father,
Alex Rosenfeld, who journeyed into the past
with me to share his inccredible experience, to
my mother, for sharing her memories,
to the memory of my brother,
Alfred Rosenfeld, and to all other
members of my family.

PROLOGUE

My father was not the only one to suffer the atrocities of WWII. His story shows us humankind at its worst, and the human spirit at its best. These pages are historical, biographical and subjective. Through the words of Alex Rosenfeld, we gain awareness of the power, courage and strength one needs to survive.

Physically and emotionally my father was a strong man. I know that because of what he taught me. He showed me his strength and taught me how to be strong. The hardship of living in a German occupied country, as a Jew, exemplifies his bravery. My father and millions of others went through similar experience. They had the power of courage, the motivation of survival at its utmost level, and the support of friends and family.

Alex, one of seven children, was born during the summer of 1916. During this time, the Russian Cossacks and the Germans set

Krakow, Poland ablaze in war. That was during WWI. Alex's family moved to Poland in the hopes of finding a better life, unfortunately, there would be no safe sanctuary there. As Hitler rose to power, the safety of Polish Jews became highly tenuous. Discrimination of the Jews had existed for hundreds of years, however, during this period of history, discrimination was legally sanctioned and Jews were forced into organized settlements. In these settlements, they toiled for hours on end with little food or rest. This put Jews in the position of having to examine their core beliefs and how they defined themselves as Jews. During this time, teens were attracted to various political movements, in order to rally support for the war. Because of his athletic prowess, Alex was able to participate in non-Jewish organizations. He was an industrious, hard working man with useful knowledge and determination. His athleticism was later thought to have contributed to his survival, as were the engineering skills he had acquired while working in his father's factory.

Adolf Hitler came to power in the 1930's. Anti-Semitism was on the rise and Jewish students were being segregated. This negatively affected both the quality of their education and any possibility of having any educational opportunities. Ironically, it was discrimination that inspired Alex, who at age 17 left Poland to undertake a program of study in France. While he was in school, World War II broke out. As the Nazis occupied France, his education and life became completely disrupted.

Parents were losing their jobs. Even Julius, Alex's brother, wrote that he could no longer send him money. Alex lost contact with his brother Alfred and eventually all communication with his family in Poland ceased. During the early part of the 1940's, Jews began to emigrate from Eastern European countries to France. The 1940's census showed that 150,000 Jews had escaped to Paris. The

Germans began controlling Jewish businesses, and the ownership of property. Jews were disallowed from serving in public offices and were barred from holding position of esteem. Personal identification cards were stamped with the label "Jewish".

Eventually German forces invaded France. Survival items, such as food and clothing, were in demand. Alex became unemployed and vulnerable. My father was compelled to go into hiding in order to survive. He was apprehended in October 1941 and sent to Germany as part of a forced labor group for two years. There, he found himself in the position of having to deny his Jewish heritage to save himself. The Nazis did not discover the fact that he was Jewish. In fact, they believed that he was French, which in all probability saved his life.

The German army became like a wild beast nipping at the heels of the French, Polish and English. People searched the globe looking for pathways to safety. Many never got to their destination, as they were killed along the way. Alex's decisions had to be made skillfully and swiftly if he were to survive. He had to determine who were his friends and who were his foes, when to speak and when to remain silent. He had to hide his fear, not only from the Nazis, but from himself.

After his escape from Germany in November 1943, my father was able to make his way to France. He went into hiding, and joined the French Resistance, which functioned as an underground-railroad helping people cross the borders into France and other countries.

As a result of the Nazi occupation and his capture, Alex experienced five years of extreme personal suffering, the loss of a substantial amount of family property, and the inability to complete his education. The worst thing imaginable happened when he lost his three sisters, a brother, his parents, and other family members and friends at the hands of Hitler. I myself could not imagine how anyone could have the vigor and determination to carry on, by as my father was an exceptional human being, he persevered against imaginable circumstances.

The suffering of my father has been shared with millions of individuals whose cultures and beliefs hold the highest values for democracy and human decency. They have all sustained loneliness, indignities, and the devastating loss of the ability to control their own destinies. It is difficult for me to believe that one man could hold such influence and position of evil to the point where the very existence of Jews and minorities were almost extinguished.

I often wonder what I would advise my own son to do in a similar situation. Would I tell him to do whatever he needed to do in order to survive, knowing full well that might mean denying his faith and beliefs? Or would I tell him to stand up for whatever he believed in despite the personal cost? How was my father able to do both? My father taught me not to give up. He expected me to have a good work ethic ("Filthy hands meant a good day's work"), and to always find the good in others.

Through me, you can hear my father, and millions of others speak. I am compelled to tell you to persevere, not to lose faith in humanity, and to value family and self-respect. His message, at its most primal level, is for all of us to know that the good of a few will always outweigh the evil of many!

During the last ten years of my father's life, he began to open up and talk about the past. At the same time, he had started to speak to the Jewish Federation about his memories of those times. When I found that out, I believed that it was time for him to speak to me as well. My father had not spoken to me about the past for many, many years. A part of me always wanted to know what was going through his mind. He had been silent about the event of the

Holocaust for what seemed decades. I wonder what exactly was consuming him, so I decided to seek it out.

My father had been working as an electrician for the University of Rochester. Back then, I was attending the same University, working diligently on my Bachelor's and Master's degrees. He would call me sometimes and ask if I wanted to have breakfast with him. I admit that there had been times when I would have liked to have stayed in bed and pass on his offer, but I guess I never did. Perhaps there was an innate feeling or voice that was telling me that I should go and listen to what he has to say. I saw this as an opportunity for me to take notes, both mental and written. It seemed as though I learned more about my father during this point in my life than at any other. As his story unfolded, I became more engrossed in the heroic testimony that he began to speak of. For four years, I took a detailed account of his history. It was these stories, accumulating over the years, which formed the window in which I was able to look back in time. I learned an incredible amount of not only what he had gone through, but more about who he is and was. The trials that he underwent during his lifetime had a profound impact on his emotions. He had seen a tremendous amount of suffering. Although he never fully admitted it, I believe that this was the reason that he refused to speak for so long. According to modern medicine, Post-Traumatic Stress Disorder (PTSD) is a disorder resulting from an unexpected and sudden negative stressful event. As a result, individuals may be in "shock" or denial of the event as it is so profound and abrupt. In retrospect, the event of WWII may have contributed to his premature death. One thing I am thankful for was the opportunity that I was given to bond closer to my father. His story was so inspiring I felt it was my duty to pass it on. It was not for me to keep.

It was Jewish Independence Day, May seventh, 1992 and my father was in the Temple Beth El. He suddenly collapsed and was rushed to the hospital.

He was pronounced dead-on-arrival.

Emergency personnel determined that he had sustained a massive heart attack. This came as a shock to me and my whole family. Ironically, he never touched a cigarette or drank an ounce of liquor in his life. Even at the age of 75, he appeared to be in excellent health. He always had a firm handshake. Typically, he maintained an upbeat positive attitude toward life.

I recall one thing my father said shortly before we moved to America. He told me, "When we get to America, I am going to put my feet up right on a desk". I believe he said this implying that we were going to live the so-called 'American Dream', although I don't really think he ever had any intentions of relaxing. My father, Alex, was a strong man physically and mentally. Because of his way of thinking, he refused to accept the fact that he was being punished when he was slaving under the German fist. He saw labor and hard work as positive aspects of life. Even under extreme and dire circumstances, he saw this as an opportunity to demonstrate to others and to himself that he was capable of accomplishing anything. That is how he lived his life and that is how he survived.

As for the millions of other individuals that died during that horrible time in history, let us pray and never forget the sacrifices that they endured. At the very least, I hope that my father's efforts positively changed the lives of the individuals around him. I hope that by demonstrating compassion and courage, he was able to bring a glimpse of peace and order in an otherwise chaotic world.

He may have died that day but his story, as well as his spirit, must be kept alive. My father agreed with the philosopher

Santayana, whom has stated, "Those who cannot remember the past are condemned to repeat it."

Many years later, I look back in retrospect and wonder why it took so long for my father to begin speaking about his past. Was he in shock from all of the inhumane injustices he was witness to? Was his mind repressing the many images of horror and pain? Surely my father, a man with such a strong conviction, would not be afraid to speak about such things... but as it turned out, that would be the case.

In reading the volumes of literature about World War II, I discovered that many Holocaust survivors frequently do not speak about their unsettling experiences until many years later. Fortunately, my father was strong enough to be able to tell me his story before he died. I think back in time and realize how lucky I was to have a father like that.

But what about all the other millions of fathers that did not have the chance to speak? Who tells their story? That is why I feel it is my duty to pass on his words. There are many individuals, even scholars that deny the events that occurred during the so-called "Final Solution". How can they think that when these truths are revealed? My father survived so that he can bear witness to an event that changed the world.

Every survivor has a story to tell. This is his.

I

an early background

In the late hours of a quiet summer evening, June 23, 1916, the sky suddenly lit up as if a million bolts of lightning had struck the city. Explosions rocked Krakow, Poland and shrapnel flew in all directions. The gunfire exchange of Russian Cossacks and Germans could be heard as the illuminated streets uncovered terrified people running in all directions. Into this turbulent and hostile environment of the First World War, Alex Rosenfeld was born.

Poland was, at that time and since 1772, partitioned and under the control of three different countries: Austria, Russia and Prussia. Indeed, during World War I, Poles were conscripted into these three different countries' armies.[1] At that time, it was especially hard for Jews to be mainstreamed within society. Patriotic movements were dangerous because the country was so divided politically. Hoping that things would get better, some Jews remained loyal to Poland while most turned to either Russia or Germany or chose a neutral position.[2]

Alex's paternal grandfather was a well liked man and a prominent businessman, not uncommon for Jews at that time.[3] Unlike the majority of the population who worked in agriculture, most Jews worked in commerce, industry, or professional jobs. Consequently, most Jews lived in cities. More specifically, most Jews in Poland lived in central and eastern cities.[4]

Alex's family in Poland.

Alex's grandfather owned and operated two commercial enterprises; one was a large lumberyard factory and the other was a flourmill. Both were situated in Grybow, Poland. Timber was one of the Polish industries that had been completely developed by Jews.[5]

Alex's grandfather also had four sons and one daughter. Alex's father, Solomon, was the second oldest. Cecilia, the sole daughter, was the youngest of the children. Joseph, the youngest of the sons, immigrated to New York at the age of sixteen and didn't want to work in his father's factories. Alexander, the next to the youngest son, became a dentist and migrated to Czernowiec in Romania. The oldest son, Emanuel, became a distinguished surgeon in the Austrian army. He died of typhoid during World War I.

Emigration was common for Polish Jews because they were unable to climb out of poverty, felt threatened by persecution, and couldn't worship as they pleased. Emigration increased at the end of the 19th century and continued at a steady rate until World War I. Then, the numbers increased substantially and more left than stayed. America, Berlin, England, France, Palestine, and Vienna were common destinations.[6] Four million Jews left Eastern Europe between the 1880's and 1924 and over three million of them went to the United States.[7]

Both of Alex's parents were very intelligent and industrious people. His mother, Helena Zimmerman Rosenfeld, was born in Bochnia, located near the famous underground salt mines of Wielierka at Grybow. She was fluent in both German and Polish. Alex's father spoke Yiddish, Polish and German.

Alex's parents had seven children, four sons (Alfred, Julius, Alex and Emanuel) followed by three daughters (Olga, Lucy, and Cecilia). Alex and Emanuel were identical twins, four years younger than Alfred and two years younger than Julius. The twins were one year older than Olga, four years older than Cecilia.

When Alex was almost five, his father moved the family to Stary Soncz hoping for a better life. Stary Soncz was a tiny hamlet that included approximately 100 Jewish families. The hamlet had a Jewish population of approximately 553, which was 12 percent of the total community of 4,770.[8] Following his own father's footsteps, Solomon bought two factories, a lumber factory and a flour mill that were situated along the Poprad River, two kilometers from Stary Soncz. They were operated by water power and steam power, which ran the machinery necessary for cutting the lumber.

15

Alex's parents and grandparents.

As with other communities across Poland, It was not uncommon for Jews to experience anti-Semitism in Stary Soncz. Also with the rise of Hitler, discrimination against Jews became more common and overt and Poland's Jewish population became increasingly worried for their safety.

Discrimination against Jews had existed for centuries. Dating back to the 1200s, there was canonical law that encouraged separate living arrangements for Jews. In the year 1267, the Church Council of Breslau (Wroclaw) passed canonical law to separate Jews from the rest of the people. The council claimed that they wanted to save the Christians from being affected by the "superstition and evil habits of the Jews. However, the clergy wasn't powerful enough to enforce its Law. [9] The Catholic Church also encouraged religious discrimination against Jews, fearing competition from their different faith.[10]

Another source of discrimination derived from the Jews' economic position. Since medieval times, nobility had invited Jews to Poland for the purpose of economic development. Jews were notably skilled as money-lenders and the Polish merchant class resented their competition. During the 1400s, it was common for highly restrictive measures to be taken against Jews.[11] Large towns such as Posen and Lvov limited the commercial activities of their Jewish merchants. Krakow went further and practically excluded its Jewish merchants from commerce. Similarly, some cities imposed restrictions on where Jewish people could live, and other cities, such as Warsaw, completely expelled all Jews.[12]

For centuries the Jews' economic position continued to be a source of discrimination. With the growth of urban manufacturing in the nineteenth century, more Christian Poles moved to the cities. This movement led to increased competition and anti-Semitism.[13]

Alex's family by the Poprad River in Poland.

Discrimination continued into the twentieth century, with many forms of discrimination legalized by the government. Mobs were allowed to smash market stalls and shops. Government branches dismissed Jewish workers. The government restricted credit for Jewish businessmen and increased taxes for Jewish merchants. Many other forms of discrimination have been documented.[14]

Ironically, Jewish people had played a major role in building up Poland's economy. They led the development of the export and import trade as well as industrial sectors including chemicals, transportation, printing and radio.[15] Statistics also showed that Polish Jews made an exceptional economic contribution. Although they only constituted about 10 percent of the population, they contributed 25 percent of the national income between 1918 and 1935.[16] In 1933, 52.5 percent of Poland's 395,000 businesses were Jewish.[17]

Stary Soncz originated as an organized Jewish settlement in the latter half of the 19th century. Most of the Jews were businessmen who sold their products to the surrounding small villages. In 1898, non-Jewish farmers rioted in Stary Soncz, forcing many Jewish businessmen from their livelihood. The farmers replaced the Jewish businesses with Polish cooperatives, leading many Jews to migrate overseas. Between 1910 and 1920, the Jewish population in Poland dropped by about 17 percent.[18]

Although there was anti-Semitism in Stary Soncz, Alex's father was well liked by the townspeople. Not only did he provide jobs for 65 to 85 people, but he was also known for supporting the community. As a successful businessman, he was involved in his community and was able to donate a large sum of money to build a local bridge.

Alex's mother was deeply religious, she went to the local synagogue fairly regularly and tried to reinforce the traditional family observance of the Sabbath and other Jewish holidays. Alex's father was less religious than his mother and only occasionally went to the Synagogue, but he commanded a great deal of respect and attention from his children. Alex's parents always reinforced the belief that all their children, especially the older ones were responsible for helping the others. Alex's father had tremendous foresight, a trait that saved their lives on at least one occasion. Alex remembers when "The Russian Cossacks, drinking and celebrating, suddenly came and banged on the door of our home in Maruna, Krakow "We had two bells on the balcony" To avoid causing any problems, my father humbly gave them food and liquor. They drank, laughed, danced, and then departed." This behavior was unusual because Cossacks were known for savagely treating oppressed people.[19]

II

alex's childhood

A lex began to attend the public elementary school in Stary Soncz shortly after his family moved from Krakow. This was notable as Jewish students hadn't always been allowed in this school. Back in 1909, Stary Soncz had 130 students in its elementary school and its shoemaker school, but none of these students was Jewish. These 130 students weren't in school when Solomon moved around 1921. Jewish children generally learned in elementary religious schools, where they sat together in one classroom studying the Torah and traditional Jewish subjects.[1] There were many such schools in Krakow, but when Solomon moved his family to Stary Soncz he was unable to find a religious school suitable for his children.

After four years of elementary school, Alex attended a high school in Nowy Soncz, as did his three brothers and his oldest sister.

High school was not required at that time, and it was not tuition- free. It was a privilege for children to attend high school.

However, in Alex's family as in most Jewish families, education was regarded as very important and was highly valued by his parents. Jewish parents thought it would lead to a higher status for their children.[2]

Nowy Soncz was a newer and larger community.[3] The high school was 9 kilometers from Stary Soncz. Alex took the train every day at 7 a.m. to Nowy Soncz and came home at 4 p.m. While in high school, Alex and his three brothers excelled in track. Indeed, they were considered to be one of the best athletes in the school. For extracurricular activities, they studied electricity and even made radios. This interwar time period brought new experiences for Jewish teens. Unlike their parents and grandparents, they found that Judaism no longer offered everything. As anti-Semitism grew, they felt a greater need for self-identity and self-esteem, and were attracted to different political movement such as Zionism, socialism and communism.[4]

In Stary Soncz, there were at least six different organizations for young people: two Jewish organizations, two Catholic organizations, one military organization, and one Fascist organization. Jewish teens in Stary Soncz had begun to join Zionist groups around the time of World War I. These groups were primarily composed of teens. By the 1930s, the Zionist youth movement expanded to offer activities such as sports, drama, and Hebrew.[5]

The fascist organization was called "Sokol" and was a Slavic gymnastic society. The Sokol members disliked Jewish people. Another political youth group known as National Radical Camp was known for organizing destruction in small towns on market days.[6] Alex was more interested in what he could do in the organization, than in what they represented at the time, so he had joined one Catholic organization, and a military organization called "Szczelec" because they permitted him to participate in sports activities even though he was only fourteen years old. As he recalled, "When a person was good at sports, almost every organization would take you."

Beginning as a young boy and throughout his high school years, Alex always helped his father at the lumber factory. Each morning, he rose at 4 a.m. and went to the factory, where he worked until it was time for school. It was common for children to help their families earn money and run their businesses.[7] Business was not easy. Alex remembered that when he was seven, in October, the Poprad River overflowed, causing the factory to be removed from its foundation. Almost all of the machinery and most of the property were damaged. His father was forced to rebuild the factory and he did on much more stable ground.

Alex had several responsibilities at the factory. One of his jobs was to turn on the boiler and heat the factory; another was to grease the machines. He recalled "I had to grease all the machines by 6 a.m. before the Polish workers came from Parcice and Cyganowice to begin their workday." Parcice and Cyganowice were towns about four kilometers from Stary Soncz. By the age of 15, Alex had acquired a lot of specialized knowledge and was able to repair all of the machinery at the plant. On the days that he didn't go to school, he worked until late at night. His industriousness paid off with more than ample funds to meet his financial needs for college.

Alex attended high school from 1925 until 1933. He did so with difficulty. For as much as he desired knowledge, he was unlike his oldest brother Alfred who graduated at the top of his class. Alex never had much for academic learning because he was more interested in the factory and spent most of his time working there. Alex enjoyed working with his hands, and indeed the time spent in the factory and working on machinery would be his life-saving grace in the future. After graduating from high school, he became a locksmith. He also passed the state examination to become a machinist specializing in steam machinery.

In 1934, the news of Hitler coming to power reached the tiny hamlet of Stary Soncz. Hitler had become a dictator and no other political parties were allowed in Germany. Indeed, the other parties' leaders were killed in a blood purge, their crime being that they had supposedly plotted against Hitler. At this time, the totalitarian police state was growing increasingly more powerful as Germany's government gained control over its people's cultural institutions, such as the press, the theater, and the arts.[8]

Now a young man at the age of 18, Alex had no misgivings about the dislike of Hitler's Germany for the Jewish people. The Germans were not the only people to be feared. In Stary Soncz and throughout Poland there were many Catholic businessmen and other people who didn't like the Jews either. This might have been because of the competition provided by the Jewish businesses, or because many Jewish employers such as Solomon had non-Jewish workers who resented having to work in a Jewish business.[9] Alex remembered vividly one particular anti-Semitic incident directed against a Jewish man who was transporting glass on his back. A member of the Fascist organization threw a rock at the man, who subsequently fell to the ground with the glass breaking all over him.

III

alex's brothers

Alex's oldest brother Alfred was good looking, tall, blond, and very strongly built. At the age of sixteen, he was said to have been able to fight several boys, one after another. When Alfred finished High School in 1931, he decided to attend Lwow University. He asked the rector where he could live, and was given the address of the "Acadamicki Dom Studenski Catholicki." Upon arriving at this address, Alfred quickly learned that many of the students discriminated against Jews. When the head of the dormitory asked him, "What religion are you?" He replied, "I m Jewish." The students thought it was a joke and laughed, because Alfred was so blond and handsome with deep blue eyes. No one would ever suspect he was a Jew. However, during his first couple of months at the dormitory, he started arousing suspicion as he was often seen in the company of other Jews. By 1932, after less than a year at the school, the Polish students started to become increasingly more intolerant of the Jewish students and made a lot of trouble for them.

A Ukrainian friend came to Alfred and said, "Unless you take your suitcase and move tonight, they'll kill you. They know you're Jewish and if you stay, the Polish students will kill you." So Alfred decided to leave the Academicki Dom Studenski Catholicki and went to another school at Zydowski Dom Studenski, but stayed in school until he left to attend the University in Lwow. At Lwow University, as at other Universities, Alfred's fears were well founded. Members of the political group "National Radical Camp" commonly used physical violence against Jewish students. [1] On one occasion in April 1932, Polish Fascist students had killed one of Alfred's best Jewish friends in school, Cele Mayer. Prejudice against Jewish students prevented them from sitting wherever they wanted. They had to sit on the left side of the classroom, the right side being reserved for Aryans. By 1937, some colleges had officialized these "Ghetto Benches." [2] Just as Jews had historically been forced to live in specially designated sections of cities, known as "ghettos," the Jewish students were forced to sit on specially designated benches.

Another incident occurred in 1935, after Alfred had been at Lwow University for three years. He and eight other Jewish students were in the library on the campus when a mob of Fascist students came to the door of the school building demanding the Jews. The mob of the Fascist students became so violent and caused such damage to the school building that the rector of the University, himself frightened of the Fascists, did not know what to do. However, Alfred and the other students refused to go outside and stood their ground. Alfred locked the door and told the rector to call the police. In response, the rector called the police. The police came with tanks and were able to disperse the Fascist students.

In May 1935, Alfred found himself alone in the middle of a field. Suddenly, around twenty five Fascist students rushed towards him. Alfred immediately drew a revolver from his pocket and declared,

"The first one to come near me, I'll kill." Not one student moved. Alfred's gun was not in fact real, but it saved him from the danger of the moment.

More forms of discrimination affected the enrollment of Jewish students. First, the Polish universities excluded Jews from those allowed to enter medical and engineering schools.[3] Gradually, these restrictions were extended to other schools, such as schools of law and philosophy.

Due to his harrowing experiences of intense prejudice and the ever-worsening prospect for Jews in Poland, Alfred left the school at Lwow in 1935 and went to Paris, France. Although he left the Lwow University before graduating he achieved honors in all of his subjects and was one of the top of his class. He could speak English, French, Greek, and Yiddish. Once in Paris, he attended school at the Sorbonne, where he studied mathematics and sciences, including physics and electricity. He was prevented from finishing at the Sorbonne because of the German invasion.

Passport of Joseph Rosenfeld. The youngest of the sons who immigrated to New York at the age of 16.

Thousands of other Polish Jews started to pursue their college education in other foreign countries, especially Czechoslovakia, France, and Italy. In 1929, 8,000 Polish Jews were attending college abroad. This was comparable to the total of 8,700 Polish Jews enrolled in Polish universities that same year. By the mid 1930s, the total number abroad decreased due to students' financial problems.[4] Back at home, these students' parents were losing their jobs due to anti- Semitism.

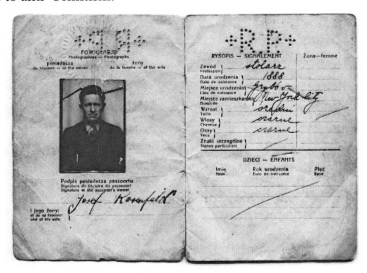

Inside Joseph's passport.

While Alfred was in France, Alex's other brothers, Julius and his twin Emanuel, served in the Polish Army. Julius entered the Polish Army in 1936. He was very strong and an excellent athlete. He first served under a good Corporal who liked him and provided him with support and encouragement. However, after three months of service, he had a different commander, a Corporal who was anti-Semitic. Within a short time, the new corporal discovered that Julius was Jewish.

One mid-May evening, someone stole an Army bell from a soldier. All the soldiers were supposed to be asleep in the barracks. However, the new Corporal told everyone, "Look for the bell."

Julius told him, "It's after 9 o'clock and we need sleep. We'll have time to look for the bell tomorrow." The Corporal replied, "You rotten, lousy Jew, shut up." Julius sprang to his feet and punched the Corporal so hard that he went reeling to the ground. Julius thought he'd killed him. After this, one of Julius's friends advised him, "It's better that you leave the army." Concerned for his own safety, Julius did just that. He deserted the army and left.

Julius returned back to his home in Stary Soncz, where his parents helped him by giving him money. By the cover of darkness, Alex took Julius's military clothing and threw it into the river somewhere between Stary Soncz and Nowy Soncz. Now Julius departed for Germany. When the Germans stopped him and asked him where he came from, Julius answered, "I came from France." Then they asked, "Where are you going?" He said, "I'm going to the Ukraine." The Germans didn't believe him and put him back on a train to Poland. However, Julius didn't go back home. He got off the train at Gdynia, Poland, and during the night he secretly boarded a ship in the harbor, not knowing where he was going. It turn out that he was not alone.

For three days and three nights, Julius hid secretly in the boat with an American stowaway. After the third night, they were so hungry and thirsty that they had no alternative but to go out onto the deck. The captain of the ship was very surprised at their presence, but couldn't remove them as they were too far out to sea. He had to allow them to remain aboard. The ship was headed from Gdynia to Uruguay in South America.

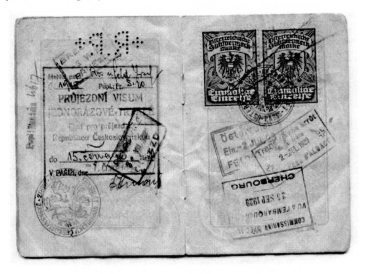

Julius was happy to arrive in Uruguay, having left Poland before the outbreak of the war. With his skills, he began working as a machinist on a Swedish ship and made several trips to New York to visit his uncle, Joseph Rosenfeld, his father's youngest brother. Julius traveled on many of these merchant marine vessels, making frequent voyages to England, Norway, Sweden, and the United States. He found his place of comfort and peace on the ocean.

Alex's twin brother Emanuel joined the Polish Army in 1937, a year later than Julius. However, in September 1939, two weeks before Emanuel was to be discharged from the army, the Germans invaded Poland. Knowing that the Germans were taking Jewish people as prisoners, Emanuel fled to Russia thinking he would be safer.

But there he was detained for seven months in prison. Eventually the Russians ordered Emanuel to be sent back to the Polish army branch at Anders in Africa. He traveled to Tehran, Iran and then to the British colony of Palestine, from where he prepared to embark to Africa. However, just before he was due to leave, he deserted the Polish Army and settled down on a kibbutz in Palestine. This is where he wanted to be. Unlike any of the brothers in the family, all of Alex's sisters remained in Stary Soncz. They wanted to stay close to home and their parents, not knowing what was coming.

IV

technical schooling in France

Due to the growing anti-Semitism, Alex knew it wasn't safe for Jews to get an education in Poland. So, in December 1936, following in his brother Alfred's footsteps, he left his family to get a college education in France. After Alex bid his father and sisters farewell, his mother accompanied him to the train station in Krakow. When he was about to board, he noticed his mother's worried face. She was crying and said, "You know Alex, I know I'll never see you again." Alex told her, "Don't be silly, I'll be back to see you again next year on my vacation." Alex boarded the westbound train. As the train was leaving, he waved goodbye to his mother and thought, "Why would she say that she would never see me again?" He traveled through Germany and on to Paris. He joined his brother Alfred, who had been living in Paris for a year.

Alex attended school at Le Alliance Francaise, located on Raispaille Boulevard. After six months, in 1937, he started school at the Sorbonne University, where his brother was also a student.

At the Sorbonne, Alex had great difficulty comprehending the more intellectual language spoken by his professors. He was good with his hands and good at working on machines, but not scholarly like his brother. Consequently, he withdrew after two months. In September, he started at a technical school known as the Ecole National des Arts et Metiers (trades) in Paris, where he was to remain for three years, until 1940. This was more in tune with Alex's interest in learning a physical, hands-on trade.

While he and Alfred were in school, his brother Julius provided him with financial assistance. Julius often wrote his brothers and planned to visit them in Paris. However, in the years they were there, he never made the trip.

During his last year of school, Alex worked part-time as a mechanic at the Olida Factory in Levalloi Perrett, a little town on the outskirts of Paris. The Olida Factory was famous for its packaged and canned meats, such as sausages and salami. While working at the factory, Alex became friends with Andre, an old World War I soldier. Alex remembered what Andre used to tell him, as he shared his old stories: "If there ever comes the time when you have the enemy before you, and you have a machine gun in your possession, never fire more than two or three bullets at any one time or they'll know your position immediately."

For some reason Alex commented, "I always remembered this all through the war, and it's quite possible that this advice saved my life."

When the Nazis invaded Poland in September 1939, beginning World War II, Julius sent Alex a letter informing him that he was no longer able to send him money. At the time, Julius was working as a seaman in the Merchant Marine in Sweden. Soon after, in what was to be his last letter ever to Alex, he expressed his innermost fears on the new war. He wrote, "This is the last trip I'm making. This job is entirely too hazardous, and if I ever get back to New York, I'll not travel by ship anymore." His last letter was sent from England. Whether he was sunk by a Nazi U boat or bombed by a plane is a matter of speculation, but he was never heard from again.

After losing contact with Julius, Alex also lost contact with Alfred. When the war started, Alex and Alfred were together on vacation in Normandy near the town of Maurice, 30 kilometers from Rouen. Alfred sensed that war in France was inevitable. So when Poland was invaded, Alfred gave Alex 1000 francs, approximately $100 in American money, and departed from France. Alfred told Alex, "I'm not joining the Army." Three days later, in October 1939, his train rumbled through Spain to Lisbon, Portugal, where he boarded a passenger ship for Argentina. He lived temporarily in Argentina and then moved to Ecuador, where he stayed.

The beginning of the war also affected many of Alex's French classmates. They were being drafted that September. However, Alex remained as a student at the Ecole National des Arts et Metiers. He made countless inquiries about his parents and sisters in Poland, but couldn't get any news. All communications with his family in Poland had ceased. He felt dispirited. No one could tell him anything about his family. He was all alone with no family to talk too, and he didn't know if his brothers were alive.

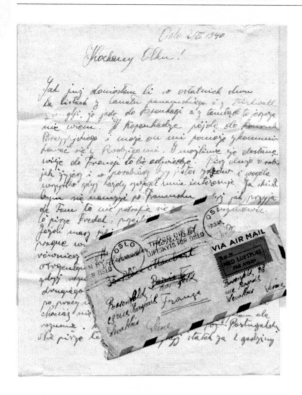

Pages 33-35 contain the final two letters and their corresponding envelopes from Alex's brother Julius who was working as a seaman in Copenhagen, Denmark.

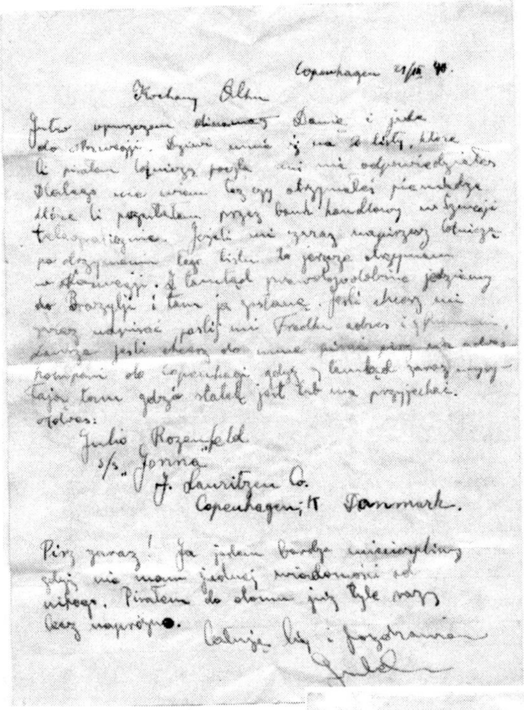

Copenhagen 29/IX 40.

Kochany Olku

adres:

Julis Rozenfeld.
s/s "Jonna"
J. Lauritzen Co.
Copenhagen K. Danmark.

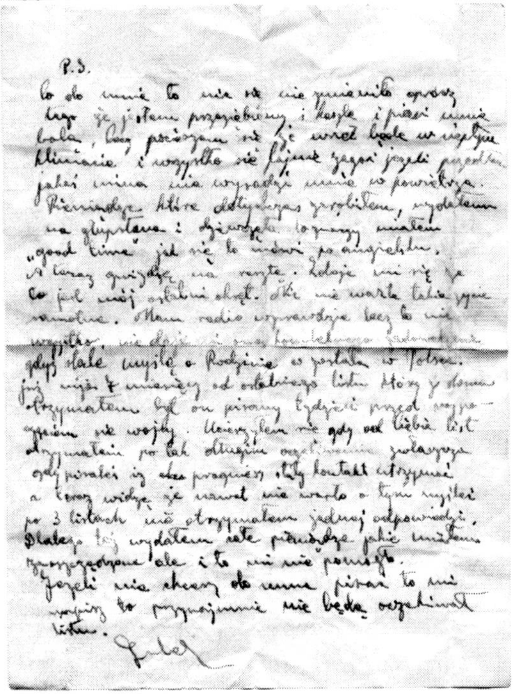

[handwritten continuation]

P.S.

[handwritten continuation]

V

---

flight to st. genole

Two weeks before the Germans occupied Paris in June 1940, Alex made an assessment of the situation and decided that the army was not the place where he wanted to be. "I sensed that if I went to the draft board, for sure I'd be killed." Several of his friends received papers to report to the draft board. Alex knew approximately when the papers would be coming for him. He decided to feign sickness and go to the hospital Hotel Dieu (translated, "God's Hotel"). The letter from the draft board did come for him at Levalloi Perrett, where he rented a small apartment. Alex informed the draft board that since his lungs were giving him much trouble, he was in the hospital Hotel Dieu for a lung check-up.

Alex left the hospital three days before the German army arrived in Paris. He packed most of his belongings, locked his apartment at Levalloi Perrett, and started his journey along the main roads due west. He could see many old people and children fleeing to avoid the Germans. His main goal was to cross the English Channel and escape to England, a goal shared by the many French soldiers after Germany invaded France.[1] Millions of the French people were fleeing southward. For many of the refugees, their goal was to reach the southwestern port of Bordeaux and then neutral Spain or Portugal. A good number of refugees were

Alex's students course vacation cards when he attended the technical school Ecole National des Arts et Metiers.

foreigners from other lands such as Belgium, Holland, and Poland. The refugees used cars, trucks, farm wagons, and even pushcarts. Many walked due to a lack of transportation or fuel. They lined the roads for hundreds of kilometers.[3] The refugees were everywhere. The roads became blocked, so traffic was moving very slowly. It was impossible for the French army to move forward.

Similarly, it was impossible for the German army to march towards Paris. To clear the roads, the Germans started to drop bombs on the civilians from above. The German planes descended like a batch of hungry vultures. As planned, the roads quickly cleared. The refugees dived for cover in the ditches and fields. The remaining cars froze due to the deaths of their drivers. Alex recalled, "As we passed one highway, the sight was horrifying. The Nazis had bombed and strafed the refugees on the highway. There was a great deal of confusion and chaos. I saw desperate people running in all direction, screaming of terror, trying to escape as their cars and belonging were burning. There were 20 to 30 burning cars and many bodies lying scattered everywhere. There were a large number of wounded and many dying, crying from pain and agony, and most were unattended. Almost all the people in the cars were killed."

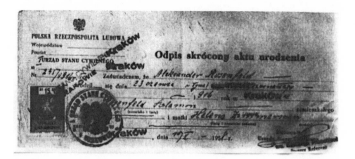

Paper believed to have come with Alex from Poland.

Those who successfully made the entire trip to Bordeaux found the boat rides to be prohibitively expensive. Money was not the only resource needed. Appropriate transit visas were required to exit through Spain. Thus, thousands of refugees sought assistance from the Portuguese Consulate in Bordeaux.[4]

At the same time as Alex's flight from Paris, British soldiers were being evacuated back to England from the beaches at Dunkirk. According to one English soldier's diary, in the course of his evacuation he saw thousands of refugees and experienced much bombing from the sky. All kinds of boats were used to transport the British troops back to England.[6] During a three-day period while Hitler's armies were moving into France, 350,000 men were successfully evacuated by boat.[7]

In July, Alex finally reached St. Genole, a little village in Brittany near the Atlantic Ocean and fairly close to England. Alex looked everywhere for boats and fisherman who could take him to England. He had an adequate amount of money and was willing to pay well for his transportation. He was able to meet some fisherman. He went fishing with them and ate a lot of sardines. When he returned to the shore, he stayed in a home of a fisherman with many other refugees.

The people in the town were very good to the refugees and

expressed much antagonism and hostility toward the Germans. Alex observed that the French people instinctively hated the Germans. Within the town, there were many male survivors from the First World War. They had shared with their families their memories of hardships and horrors at the hands of the Germans during that war.

Alex's medical certificates.

While in the town of St. Genole, Alex didn't receive any good news. He couldn't get a boat to England or anywhere else. The Nazi planes were bombing and gunning down any vessel that entered the English Channel. Numerous fishing boats were sunk and countless of people had drowned. Furthermore, the small boats couldn't make the trip in one night. Travel to England became much too risky an adventure. Tired and despondent, Alex realized that he had no choice, but to return to his temporary home in St. Genole and start planning his next move. After much contemplation, he decided to return to Paris.

While he was traveling back to Paris, the Germans invaded Paris. Alex remembered the irony of how this invasion took place less than one year after France had invited Germany to observe her military parade. The occasion was France's national holiday on July 14, 1939 (Quatorze Juillet), when France celebrated the 150th anniversary of her revolution. The German observers, however, were less interested in celebrating a nation's independence from tyrannical kings and dictators than in acquiring free information of the French military strength,[8] [9] information that would help them break through the Maginot Line by May 1940 and occupy three-fifths of France by June 22 of that year. [10] [11]

 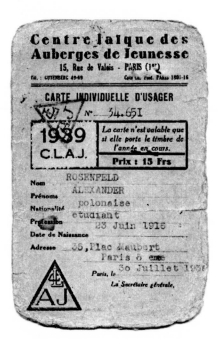

Alex's identification card in the French organization similar or equivalent to the YMCA in the United States.

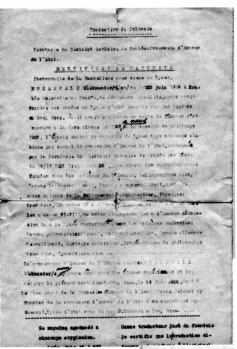

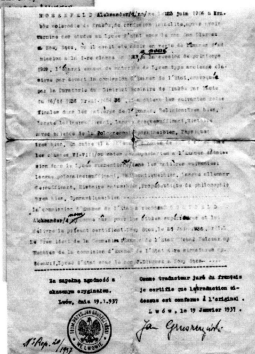

French translation from Polish. Letter from the School Board District, Krakow, provided to Alex to take with him to France describing his academic status in Poland.

VI

return to Paris

When the Germans invaded France in June 1940, they occupied France's Atlantic coast and the northern area, from
Geneva in Switzerland almost to Tours. They left the southern portion under the control of Marshal Petain, who collaborated with
the German Army. The Nazis imposed very rigid controls on all
movements between occupied France and the "free-France" zone.

In the free France zone, Petain immediately began a program of
indoctrinating the French soldiers. Unoccupied France, governed
from Vichy, became a fascist state.[2] Special stamped permission
and papers from the Germans were required for anyone wishing to
move between free France and German-occupied France. People
who passed illegally were sent to prison or were killed.[3]

When beginning his journey back to Paris in July 1940, Alex
met a family, three women, a man, and two children, who wished
to return to Paris as well. Since Alex had his driver's license, he told
them that he'd drive them to Paris if they were willing to pay him

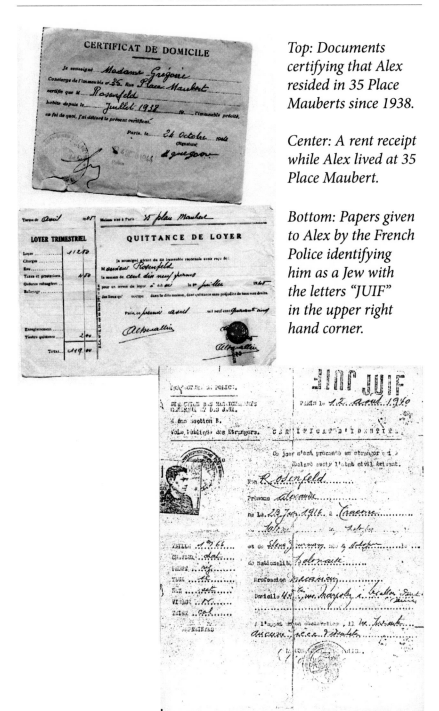

Top: Documents certifying that Alex resided in 35 Place Mauberts since 1938.

Center: A rent receipt while Alex lived at 35 Place Maubert.

Bottom: Papers given to Alex by the French Police identifying him as a Jew with the letters "JUIF" in the upper right hand corner.

for his services. They agreed to pay for his food along the journey as well.

The roads to Paris were not blocked as they had been when he fled to St. Genole. Later, Alex was to hear how many other civilian refugees to the north were butchered along the roadways. He discovered that the Germans had killed thousands on their way to Paris, using Stuka bombers to kill men and women, old and young alike.

When Alex arrived in Paris, he couldn't believe what he saw. He found the city empty and couldn't find anyone in the streets. Restrictions were being enforced, including an evening curfew for the general population.[4]

Apart from the curfew, the Germans didn't concern themselves much with the civilian population in Paris during the first three weeks of occupation. Elderly individuals could go out and return to their homes as long as they had special stamped permission from the German army.

Alex didn't know what to do when he returned back in Paris. He talked to several French people who provided him with limited options. He cautiously evaluated the situation in Paris and decided to go to the French police and tell them he was a Frenchman. In this way he could have his paper stamped at this time. He was running short of money, and transportation and movement in the city were becoming extremely difficult.

Alex had the choice of two places to live. He could go back to his apartment at Levalloi Perrett or get a room somewhere in Paris. Since Levalloi Perrett was about 24 kilometers from Paris and things were becoming increasingly more dangerous, he decided to stay in Paris. He took a room at 35 Maubert Place, a 700-year-old house. He had great neighbors who never gave him any troubles. One particular neighbor was Mr. and Mrs. Sally. They had a daughter name Eva, whom Alex liked very much because of her generosity, charm and beauty. Alex recalled, "Eva had beautiful long brown hair and was very beautiful. However, she was only fifteen years old and too young for Alex. Mr. and Mrs Sally and Eva provided Alex with any assistance they could, spending many hours teaching him new French words. They also taught him good French cooking. Alex no longer had a sense of being safe and was almost always in a state of agitation, anticipating the presence of danger.

Another identification document.

Two weeks after his return to Paris from St. Genole, Alex started to look for a job. Finally, he found one at 90 Rue Rochechoir, the Fortex Factory where spring were manufactured. Alex worked at the factory as a mechanic, repairing, changing, and rebuilding machines.

In Paris Alex sometimes visited his cousins, Clara and Israel Erdman, who lived at 18 Rue de L'Etoile. The Erdman family originally came to Paris from a small town in the Ukraine. At first they moved to Berlin, where they operated an eggs-and-butter grocery business. When Hitler came to power, they decided to move to Paris.

In Paris, the Erdmans also operated another eggs-and-butter grocery business, similar to their previous store in Berlin. The

Paris business was located at 17 Rue D' Enghen. Alex often visited them at home or at their business when he got off from work.

Alex had another cousin in Paris, whose name was Schenkman. Schenkman was 65 years old and a dentist by profession. He originally lived in Romania, but had moved to France 40 years earlier. All of his children were born in France. Schenkman's son was also a dentist and two daughters still lived in Paris. Schenkman had a laboratory and clinic in the Belleville section of Paris and his son Leo had a clinic at Montmartre. They were both prosperous. The Shenkmans owned a huge estate approximately 20 kilometers from Paris.

Before the war, Alex often visited the Schenkman's at their villa on Sundays and he would sometimes stay for the weekend. They were very supportive toward him. However, when the war started, it became too risky to visit them and so Alex never saw them again.

The Schenkmans also had an apartment in Paris. On one occasion, the entire family went away leaving behind their 16-year-old daughter Jacqueline. One day, three German officers came to the apartment and demanded that Jacqueline open the door, which she did at once. One officer asked, "Where are your parents?" to which she replied, "They're not home. They went away for the day."

The German officer didn't take her. However, on departing, he said to her, "If your parents come back here before nightfall, tell them that we want to talk with them and will come back tonight to see them"

When her parents did return during the evening and heard this news, they knew that they would be arrested if they stayed. They heard that the Germans were starting to arrest Jews. They all hurriedly left, taking with them the barest necessities. They left most of their belongings behind as they tried to get away from Paris and escape to southern France. The only member of their family who remained in Paris was the Schenkman's son Leo. He had been living in Paris with his 21-year-old French girlfriend during the German occupation and stayed with her throughout the entire war. After the war, Leo confided in Alex and told him, "Throughout the war I was always worried, because my girlfriend and her family could have sold me out to the Germans, but they never did."

In September 1940, a Jewish doctor named Andre became friends with Alex. He asked Alex if he could room with him because he had no other place to live. Alex consented to this, as Andre was willing to pay a portion of the rent. They soon became good friends. Also in September, an ordinance was established by the Germans, requiring a census of all Jews in the Occupied Zone.

Jewish people were also ordered to register at their local police station and indicate their home address, nationality, and profession. [6][7] As of May 1940, there were 350,000 Jews in France. Half of them had recently emigrated to escape the Germans. Furthermore, half of France's Jewish population lived in Paris.[7]

As of October 1940, there were 150,000 Jews in Paris.[8] The census showed that 80% of the foreign Jews came from Eastern Europe, with the largest group coming from Poland.[9] In October 1940, the Germans were not yet taking the Jews captive. However, the Germans began imposing economic decrees upon the Jewish people that hurt them financially. Jewish businesses were no longer allowed to operate and had to be turned over, to non-Jewish administrators. Jews were no longer allowed to own any property and could no longer hold public service positions. Jews were also beginning to lose positions in liberal professions such as medicine and law.[10]

In October, Alex lost a good friend, Altman, who was an active member of the French Paris underground. Altman was a former student friend and a doctor, who was doing his internship at Hotel Dieu, one of the hospitals in Paris.

One day, the Nazis came and set up a roadblock between Rue Des Ecouffe and Rue d'Elm where Altman and his group were located. The Nazis closed the other streets and encircled Altman's building. Since Altman's men had plenty of ammunition, scattered all over on the floor, they were confident that they could hold off the Germans for some time. However, it was impossible to hold them off indefinitely. Just as in the case of the Warsaw Ghetto, the Germans realized that they couldn't take Altman and the members of his group alive, and indeed they didn't desire to do so. However, the German soldiers decided to storm the house and they shot Altman and his friends. This eliminated Altman's underground organization.

In November, Alex and his doctor friend Andre each received a letter from the French Commissariat of Police requesting them to report to the police station. They were very anxious as they arrived at the police station. A sergeant was seated behind an empty desk. He requested their identification cards and other papers that furnished information on their legal status. Alex presented his

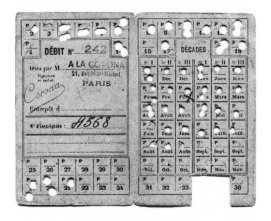

Tobacco ration cards used to buy tobacco.
Alex would trade this to purchase food.

identification card and other documents. The sergeant discretely examined Alex's identification card and then very swiftly stamped "Jewish" on his identification card as well as on others of his papers.

Alex commented on this occurrence, "The nervous French policeman put the first stamp on upside down and consequently had to turn the papers over and stamp the other side the proper way. As a result, I ended up with two stamps on my identification card instead of one."

Similarly, the sergeant placed a "Jewish" stamp on Andre's identification card as well. After work, Andre told Alex, "It's impossible for me to remain in Paris now. I'll have to leave and can't stay here. I'm going to southern France." Within several days, he fled south and Alex never heard from him again.

Many of Alex's former friends were killed during the occupation. One of them, Bernard Warsow, tried to escape when the Nazis came to his home in the country outside of Paris. He was gunned down crossing the road outside his home.

By November 1940, it had become increasingly difficult for people to get enough to eat. The German occupation forces consumed the majority of the market's food supplies. Similarly, they used a large percentage of all the supplies, leaving shortages in all daily needs, ranging from flour to coal. Consequently, for the next five years each person was given a ration card. These cards were to be used for everything, including groceries such as bread and meat, clothing, and coal. [11]

The Germans decreed was that there would be food and clothing allowances for each person. However, this did not provide sufficient rations to meet peoples' basic needs. The German also did not distribute the goods fairly. [12] The food rations were too little, especially for Alex, who was strong, active and accustomed to eating large portions. Fortunately, Alex became friends with his boss Richard at the

Fortex Factory. Richard's family was extremely wealthy, having been in business for a very long time. They were Jewish and had migrated to Paris from Rome, Italy. Richard had three brothers living in Paris. Richard's family had saved a good supply of cheese that they were receiving from relatives in Italy and they were willing to share their cheese with Alex. Their generosity saved him from starvation. He was able to survive well while the factory remained in operation and while he was in contact with Richard.

However, Richard and his family had suffered much during the war. His mother and other family members were captured by the Germans and never returned. Alex observed that at first, the Germans took only the elderly Jews. The younger ones were more agile and could more easily escape, which made it difficult for the Germans to hold them. Alex also noted that the elderly Jews never returned.

In January 1941, Richard was so frightened of the Germans that he closed down the factory. He was afraid that the German Gestapo or soldiers would be coming for him as well. With the factory closed, Alex suddenly found himself among the hungry and unemployed. Of this dramatic change in his situation, Alex recalled, "I became very disheartened and discouraged. "I didn't have much money left at this time, I had no job, and I couldn't move without money or without endangering my very life."

VII

the black market

In order to survive, Alex knew he had to act swiftly. He was forced to go into the black market. He went to one of his Jewish friends named Federgrin, who was also a good friend of his cousin, Israel Erdman. Federgrin was already involved in the black market. Black market dealings involved Jews and the non-Jewish alike. However, Jews were disproportionately blamed for black market activities.

People turned to black market dealing as an alternative for survival, because the rations provided were simply insufficient. Indeed, one survival technique was to forge ration cards.[1]

Meanwhile, due to the food shortage, Erdman sold his grocery business and bought a restaurant. It was located near the Anghen Street area where most businesses were Jewish. Due to the state of the economy, most people couldn't afford to eat in restaurants. Thus, Erdman was also forced into the black market business. He used his restaurant's back room as a place to conduct black market transactions, selling leather products and various other items, such as belts, wallets, and jackets.

Alex and Federgrin assisted Erdman by buying chocolate and sugar in large quantities. Using their addresses of people craving these supplies, they went with their truck to make deliveries. Erdman was scared to go on these trips. He prepared the supplies and arranged the business, but never made the deliveries. Alex remarked about his new occupation, "Personally, I never liked this job but I was able to make good money. I was always fearful, however, that the French police would spot us."

Alex knew that there was no other way to survive. Sometimes he was given a small job to do, working as a plumber or an electrician or whatever else was available at the time. He felt lucky when he could work two or three hours in a day. The black market thus occupied the majority of his time. Alex would buy goods that he could sell in the black market. He would go to the Olida factory at Levalloi Perrett and buy some conserves (canned meats). Sometimes the salesman there would give him 20 boxes of conserves and sometimes 30. Alex paid the normal price for the goods but received a much bigger price for them on the black market.

Alex remembered how scattered small-arms fire and explosions could spasmodically be heard throughout various areas of Paris. Sometimes in the subways at night it was easy for the French to kill one or two German soldiers out alone. However, when these isolated incidents occurred, the Germans retaliated by randomly rounding up French people and shooting them in the squares.

Alex heard gunfire beginning in April 1941 and every night thereafter. He was very cautious about his movements and actions at all times. He recalled, "I always tried to be home before 12 midnight because of the grave danger of the early morning hours. In particular, old people caught out on the street after midnight were killed." Alex slept at his 35 Maubert Place apartment.

During the day, Alex always wore dirty working clothes instead of clean clothes so that he could move about without attracting any suspicion, to make it less likely that the police would catch him. When Alex traveled through the streets, he would often see the police apprehending someone else but he was able to avoid detection. Alex traveled by bicycle. He was afraid to travel by subway because the police maintained a very rigid control of subway travel. He felt very fortunate that the police didn't stop him or ask him for his papers.

That spring, the Germans started to expel or intern Paris's foreign Jews. They were arrested before the French Jews. Since the unoccupied zone didn't desire any more Jews, the Germans instructed the police to intern them. On May 14, 1941, over 3,700 male foreign Jews received summons.[2] After that date, there was a continual stream of arrests.[3] To protect themselves, Jewish immigrants tried to obtain false identity papers.[4]

Alex remembered one night in June 1941, when a German soldier was killed by a Frenchmen. The Germans retaliated by killing between 100 and 200 French hostages and placing billboards on the street the next day showing the names of the French dead.

By October 1941 there was a decree, "Code des hotages," stating that for every German killed by the French the Germans would shoot 50 to 100 hostages.[5] Alex remembered one night in October when he saw the Nazis marching with 300 hotages. The next day it took him almost one whole hour to read the names of those who had been killed that night. In his opinion, "These Nazi massacres and butcheries were useless." The Germans tried to frighten the French people, but they underestimated the depth and bitterness of the resentment that their "Code des hostages" engendered. The more French civilians they killed, the more they united and intensified the French resistance. "The French are a very patriotic people," Alex remarked.

Erdman, Federgrin, and Alex continued their involvement in the black market throughout the spring and summer months of 1941. They also started a business of buying and selling gold for American dollars. The American dollar was a valuable commodity. Alex was making more money than ever before. From two truckloads of sugar, he could earn enough money to live for two weeks. The older Jewish people knew and trusted Alex, probably because of his aunt and uncle Clara and Israel Erdman, who had many friends in the city.

However, The Germans slowly started to close in on their business. One summer day in June 1941, two German businessmen came to the Erdmans' house, claiming that they were friends. The Erdmans didn't know whether they were Gestapo agents or whether they were telling the truth. Little by little, other strangers began infiltrating or trickling into the area. The elderly Jews began to grow more fearful and restless. At this same time, the Germans requested a contract with the Erdmans and other Jewish businesses to make winter coats and other winter clothing for the German army. Some Jewish people profited from this contract.

Alex's luck began to change. It became increasingly difficult to obtain the canned meat. Every time he went to the Olida factory, they gave out less, until, finally, the Germans took control of the factory. Alex went to the factory and they gave him nothing, telling him, "Nobody can give any more."

In the late summer of 1941, the Germans started to pick up Jewish people and take them away to Drancy, a concentration camp not far from Paris. Drancy, one of three such concentration camps in France, was an unfinished housing complex converted in 1941 to serve as an internment camp for Jews.[6] Drancy was known for having inadequate lodgings and supplies for the inmates. At one point there were only 1,200 wooden bunk-bed frames for

4,000 Jews. There were also inadequate supplies of daily necessities such as food and toiletries. Local French authorities didn't want to take responsibility for improving the accommodations, claiming insufficient funds. Consequently, many health problems developed and lice, dysentery, and diarrhea were common. It was difficult to escape from this camp.

Alex's friend Federgrin, a Polish Jew, was captured and placed in confinement at Drancy. While Federgrin was driving home one evening in September 1941, the Germans closed the street and caught him. The Jews weren't the only ones arrested; those who couldn't present their identification cards were also arrested. Once in the autumn of 1941, Alex was riding down the street on his bicycle when he passed by a long line of 200 to 300 elderly men, women, and children marching in single file into boxcars or trains bound for Drancy.

Even larger mass arrests began that winter. In December, during one of France's first mass arrests of Jews, 1,000 Jewish professionals and intellectuals were taken.[7] By December 1941, approximately 8,000 Jews had been arrested and sent to one of four different camps.[8]

While at Drancy, Federgrin, who was strong and intelligent, managed to escape by sneaking out under the barbed wire one evening. He was recaptured, he escaped again, and was recaptured a second time. Alex visited him and found that he had become exceedingly angry.

Federgrin told Alex how a young man, 22 or 23 years old, tried to escape. He was an exceptional athlete, good at the high jump. He decided to take advantage of his ability at pole-vaulting, which he had learned in school. The barbed wire was a serious obstacle as it was very high, possibly over 7 meters! He thought he could spring over and clear the topmost wire. Everyone had attempted it without high-jumping experience had perished, and many had tried in vain.

One evening, when it was dusk, this athlete took his pole and made a lunge over the wire, but his clothing hooked onto the top wire and the German soldiers opened up with rifle fire. "There he was," Federgrin said to Alex, "Just hanging limp on the top wire. He almost made it. He just missed, and when he missed the Germans finished him off." Federgrin told Alex that he would try to escape from Drancy again. Whether Federgrin ever did is not known, as Alex never heard from him or about him again.

It was difficult and dangerous for Alex to move about. No one knew when the police would catch anyone. In November 1941, Alex was riding his bicycle after midnight. Because he didn't take the necessary precautions, two French gendarmes (policemen) on bicycles intercepted him and took him into custody. He was then interrogated at the police bureau. Alex was frightened beyond description, and was told by one policeman, "Don't move from here, any time now the German patrol will be passing down the street. You wait here until morning." Alex slept on the bench at the police bureau until 5 a.m. Two policemen abruptly awakened him and told him, "You can go home now." They also told him, "This is the last chance you get, No more warnings."

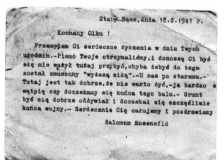

The final postcard that Alex received from his father from Poland.

VIII

assignment and reception of working apers

In November 1941, Alex received a letter requesting him to report to the French Bureau d' Emploiment in Paris. Apparently, the French police had misplaced his registration from the previous year when he had registered as a Jew. When he arrived, the French police were inside, seated at their desks. They questioned Alex, "Where do you work?" He replied, "I'm not working at present, but I have worked at the Fortex Factory." Alex was puzzled. They had never previously cared whether he worked, and they had never before tried to get work for him.

The French policemen in command then spoke and said, "Rosenfeld, you know we have to send all Frenchmen from 18 to 45 to Germany to work. You know we don't like to send our own people. You're a stranger among us. We don't want to send you either. But let's face it, this is war and we'd prefer to send you before our own people."

After their long conversation, they gave Alex his alimentation card, his food ticket for two weeks. If Alex didn't go to Germany, he couldn't get an alimentation card after the two weeks. He knew that without food he wouldn't be able to survive. He had no other option but to tell them, "All right, I'll go." They gave him several days to get his clothing and arrange his affairs. All in all, the police at the employment office were very hospitable and friendly. They gave him the address of the German Bureau in Paris where he was to report for his working papers.

Due to its wartime labor shortage, Germany drafted civilian workers and prisoners of war from France, Russia, Poland, Belgium, and many other countries.[1] In 1942, the Germans were encouraging Frenchmen to volunteer for German factories. When there weren't enough volunteers by 1943, the Germans began compulsory labor.[2] Between 1939 and 1945, Germany deported over 10 million people to become forced laborers.[3] Most German companies used this labor during World War II.[4]

About three or four days later, Alex went to visit his cousins, Israel and Clara Erdman, and told them what had been happening with him, and that he would be going to Germany to work in factories. He told them that the black market was far too hazardous, and that, even though he had obtained an alimentation card from the French Bureau d'Emploiment, he didn't have enough money left to buy the food he needed to survive. Alex also told them he couldn't go to southern France because the control was too strict at Vierzon.

Alex's cousins then said "You better go and register at the Jewish office like they've ordered." Alex replied in anger, "Never. I'll never do this. I'll never go there, that is insanity. They'll catch me too easily and quickly if I go there. Besides, I have to have the yellow band on my shirt or coat marked Juif (Jew). I will definitely not sit on the last wagon in the subway." Although the consequences for not wearing the Jewish mark could include internment, Alex was not alone in his protest.[5]

Jews in France were required to wear a yellow band with a Jewish mark of the Star of David on the top of their coats or shirts. Although it didn't become an official decree until June 1942, the rule was in effect by 1940.[6] [7] Poland had similar decrees that were instituted much earlier, the first being in Lodz on November 12, 1939.[8]

Germany was unable to enforce an armband decree in Denmark. After Germany invaded Denmark in 1940 and tried to identify the Jews with armbands, the Danish people successfully resisted. Following the example of King Christian X, almost everyone wore the armband in protest. Consequently, the Germans ended this requirement in Denmark.[9] In addition to wearing armbands, Jews in France were required to sit on the last wagon of subways. It was very easy to trap many Jews at one time because of these rules. At first, not very many Jews put the yellow bands and marks on their clothing. Many of those who did were seized by the Nazis and shipped on trains and trucks to concentration camps. In July 1941, Drancy received 6,000 internees, many as a result of these rules.[10]

Alex did not follow his cousins' advice. Refusing to go to the Jewish office, he went instead to the German Employment Bureau and showed the papers that he had received from the French Bureau d' Emploiement. The Germans behind the desk spoke good French, not fluent, but more than adequate for normal conversation. There were many German officers, seated at every other table. First they meticulously reviewed Alex's papers. One officer looked up at Alex and, staring straight into his eyes, barked rudely and abruptly, "Rosenfeld, Alexander Rosenfeld. Where were you born? Where did you come from?" Alex responded, "I came from Poland." The German officer then demanded, "Well, where is your passport?"

By this time Alex was frightened. He did have his passport, but pondering the situation and moving cautiously, he again responded, "Sir, when I was in the Army, I never got my documents. I only received a temporary document from the prefecture. The Army still has my document." The first officer stepped aside to speak privately with a second, older officer. The older officer came striding forward, moved to Alex's side, examined the profile of his face, and circled to his other side, again studying his face. Alex knew German, but when they asked if he knew German, he denied it. The older German officer then asked Alex, "Are you a Jew?" Alex again replied, "No." He then asked, "What religion are you?" to which Alex replied, "Roman Catholic."

Finally, taking one last look from the side, the older officer said to the other officer, "Nein, das is nicht Jude!" Translated, this means, "No, he is not a Jew!" Again turning to Alex, one of the officers asked, "In what profession or trade are you skilled or proficient?" Alex replied, "My profession is as a mechanic." The older officer said, "Look, we have places to which we can send you, but do you know aluminum work?" Alex replied, "Yes, I know aluminum work very well." The officer nodded. "We have two places we can send you." Turning to a huge map of Germany, he pointed to one place near the Polish border and a second in Bremen.

They told him he would be making the same money at Bremen as the German workers, and every three months he would be permitted to return to France for three days. He was then asked, "Where would you rather go?" Alex replied, "I will go to Bremen, because it's closer to France." Alex wasn't interested in going anywhere near the Polish border as it was possible that someone might know him there. After the officers wrote down all of his answers, they gave Alex his papers to go to a medical building for a physical examination.

Two days later, Alex went for this exam. The Germans wouldn't take anyone suspected of being sick to work in their factories. They took only the healthy; hence, it was necessary and routine procedure for Alex to be examined. He climbed to the second floor where he saw at least seven or eight doctors and many people waiting in long lines. Alex got in line and went first to a German specialist for eyes, next to one for ears and throat, then to a third for lungs, and so forth. When he went to the lung doctor, he was instructed to undress. The doctor saw him, healthy and strong, and said, "In which sport do you participate?"

Alex responded, "Doctor, it's from hard work, not athletics. I work hard." The German lung specialist put his hand behind Alex and began to tap him repeatedly. This doctor had examined many people before Alex, but was struck by something unusual. He told Alex, "You're so strong and muscular. I've never seen such a handsome, beautiful, strong Frenchman before." Finally, Alex saw the doctor who was testing whether he and the other potential workers had a venereal disease. Alex was given his papers and directed to the German Employment Bureau, where he would be instructed on what to do next.

Alex returned to the Bureau, handing the result of his physical examination to the German officer. Seeing that Alex had passed, the officer gave him three sets of papers, including one for the zugfurer (train conductor). Alex was told to report promptly to the train bound for Bremen the next morning.

IX

journey to a new home and job

That next morning in November 1941, Alex reported to the train the Gare du Nord in Paris for departure to Bremen. "I had to board Train 13," Alex commented. "The French people believed 13 was a very good number." Alex looked around and saw that there must have been 400 to 500 people on this train alone. Each car held an identical number of people. They took his three papers after he boarded the train. Alex's compartment had about 20 people, so there was plenty of space available for sleeping. However, the travelers were too anxious to be able to sleep. It was to be a much-delayed one-week train ride to Bremen. Every five or six hours, the train stopped at various towns along the way. Usually, a German woman or a lady from the Red Cross Society would serve black coffee, bread, and sometimes one hamburger. The elderly French people took their own food, sometimes for an itinerary as long as two or three weeks.

While in France, the train seldom moved very much during

the day. The engineer was terrified that the train would be bombed from the air by the British Air Force, and so the train moved mainly at night. Alex remained in one compartment for most of the trip. In his compartment were three young Frenchmen and one French girl, aged about 20, who had a boyfriend in Germany. She was going there to visit him. Alex talked to the girl most of the first day.

When the train arrived in Hanover, Germany, everyone was very tired, but the travelers were told that it was necessary for all the passengers to change trains. The Germans motioned for everyone to go inside a big house where there were big rooms for transients and travelers. At this time of the year, no one could stay outside because the weather was terrible. It was near zero and snowing. All the passengers had to wait until 11:30 a.m. the next morning for their next train.

Alex was awakened the next morning by the shrieking screams of a German officer. All the people were ordered into the center of a large hall. The German officer had found excrement on a portrait of Hitler and had become exceedingly enraged. Alex suspected that some Frenchman had done it the previous evening.

After all the people were assembled, the officer shouted, "I must know the man that did this; put your hand up." For several minutes, there was nothing but silence. The officer again screamed more vehemently both in French and in German, demanding that the person's identity be known. Again the officer shouted, "Who did this? I must know the man that did this." After a couple more minutes of silence, he made a speech in French. "Where do you think you are, in France? You're in Germany now, this is a clean country, and we won't tolerate actions like this here." Alex was frightened. The officer then motioned to eight people. "You...you... you and you...go and clean this," whereupon the eight assigned people went and reluctantly cleaned up the mess.

When the train finally arrived in Bremen, the workers first had to go to the Gestapo office. The Germans then escorted everyone to a large school where the people were assigned to different factories. Each factory had its own lodging for its own workers. At the big school in Bremen, everyone was directed to put their baggage where there was available space, and then was told to report for duty at an office building near the school.

At the school, Alex stayed in Room #14 on the second floor. There were about 15 beds in every room. Alex spent the first evening with Belgians who came from Flanders. They were very kind people; Alex lived with them through January 1942. Alex put his belongings and clothing in a wooden closet in Room #14 and placed his suitcase under his bed. The Belgian people wanted to know where he came from. Alex told them, "I came from France." Alex was afraid that they would ask him too many questions but they didn't ask many more.

When Alex arrived at the office building near the school, he acted as though he didn't know even one word of German. There was a Belgian interpreter in the office and a German woman who did the interrogating. The German woman threw many different questions at Alex. The interpreter translated what Alex said for the German woman. First they asked his name, address, place and date of birth, and so forth. Finally the German woman asked Alex his nationality. Alex answered, "Francais." "What were your parent's names?" she questioned. Alex replied, "Rosenfeld. I was born during World War I and I never knew my father and mother; I was an orphan.

"Other people took care of me; their name was Rosenfeld. My real parents died in the first war." As the Belgian interpreted his words, the German woman wrote all of this down on paper. Next, Alex was asked his profession. He told them, "I' m a mechanic by trade. I do chiefly metal work." They then proceeded to tell him that he would be sent to an airplane factory in Bremenburg, about 8 kilometers from Bremen.

The Germans gave Alex an alimentation card for one week's food. The food portion was much too small for Alex. He was also given a transportation card for the electric streetcar. When Alex returned to the school the same day, he went directly to his room and arranged his things. At 7:00 p.m. that evening, he went to eat dinner.

The German supervisor asked for his ticket and removed one piece from the card. That first evening, Alex was provided soup, as would be the case every evening, and he was given his weekly allotment of food that he was to store in his room. He was given four or five pounds of bread, 80 grams of margarine, and a half glass of sugar. The Flemish people were puzzled by Alex because, as a rule, everyone tended to stay with their own ethnic group. Alex was an exception, everyone thought that he was either anti-social or a loner.

One Belgian asked Alex, "Why don't you stay with the Frenchmen?" Alex replied, "I' m quiet. I like to be by myself." This same man said, "Aw, you're not really a Frenchman, you wouldn't stay with us if you were." Alex was angered by this remark and exclaimed, "If you don't like it, I'll go to another room." At this the Belgian remarked, "I was only joking, you can stay here with us as long as you like. We're glad to have you." After that, they never bothered him again.

X

the factory at Bremenburg

Alex worked at the factory in Bremenburg that was called Algeme Wesser Flugzaigbau. It was a very small factory that was affiliated with the main factory in Bremen. Alex's job was to help assemble stukas (dive bombers). More specifically, Alex helped make copper pipes to hold the gasoline in the stukas. There were approximately 100 of these copper pipes in each plane.

When Alex reported to the factory, he was sent to Meister Mudh, his supervisor. Meister Mudh asked Alex if he spoke German. Alex gave a negative reply, saying, "I don't know German, but I'll try my best to learn."

Initially at the factory there were five Germans and a short Frenchman named Louis, but known as Napoleon by the Germans and Alex. There was also another man, from the Ukraine whose, name was Phil Hawrilo. All the Germans at the factory had specialized as welders and pipe fitters and were experts in machinery repair. One of the Germans named Mueller asked Alex, "Do you know pipe work?" Alex replied that he did. Then Mueller said, "You'll work with me. I'll ask Meister Mudh."

Mueller and the other Germans taught Alex welding and how to work with all the machinery. After a week, Alex was able to repair just about all of the machinery by himself. Meister Mudh was then able to send Alex to all parts of the factory, inside and out, whenever machinery had broken down and needed repair.

Back at the school in Bremen, Alex encountered Herr Reinicke, a civilian. Reinicke was the lager fuhrer, the person responsible for all the lodging at the school. Alex remembered one occasion when Reinicke acted in a dictatorial manner. A Frenchman named Rondo was sick one morning and stayed in bed instead of going to work. When Reinicke found him in bed, he began to argue furiously with him. Reinicke's temper got the best of him and he punched Rondo in the face. When Napoleon came to Rondo's assistance, Reinicke pulled out his gun and hit Napoleon over the head with the butt of his revolver.

Alex liked the two Frenchmen Rondo and Napoleon very much, but the Germans didn't care for either of them. Within three days, the Germans had sent Rondo to another place to work. Napoleon told Alex, "I will not stay here. I hate their guts. Why should I work here and take this nonsense? I'm going to go back to France." After the incident with Reinicke, Napoleon did his work so grudgingly that after a few months he was intensely disliked by his German co-workers. He would do exactly the opposite of what he was instructed to do. Consequently, he caused such a lag in production that by March, the supervisor at the factory, Meister Mudh, sent him elsewhere to work.

Alex remembered another example of Reinicke's behavior. During a bombing alert, barracks began to burn. All the workers were ordered to change barracks. The bombs struck closely by, again and again. More barracks started burning, so the workers escaped to the bunkers.

Meanwhile, Reinicke secretly sneaked into the barracks and stole all the money he could find. One worker named Simon didn't go to the bunkers and hid when he saw Reinicke come into the barracks. Simon watched Reinicke take the money. When Reinicke was questioned about stealing the money, he told authorities, "The money burned during the bombing raid." But Simon claimed he saw Reinicke steal the money. The police were called in, and they found Reinicke with the money. Alex later asked someone why he hadn't seen Reinicke around lately, and one of the German workers responded, "Reinicke's in prison."

In February 1942, Alex was sent to one part of the factory where pipes for stukas were made. He saw that all the people there had a yellow piece of cloth marked "P" for Polish.[1] There were approximately 400 Polish workers in this section. Some were riveters, while others applied the torches and bent the copper pipes. When the rivet machines broke down, Alex was instructed to repair them.

The Polish people were very friendly towards Alex. He told them that he spoke French, but he didn't tell them that he had been born in Poland. Alex was able to communicate with several Polish men who knew a little French. There were several other Polish workers who spoke German but were not fluent.

While Alex was in this section of the factory, he discovered that one machine had a defective sponge. Alex went to Meister Mudh and reported that a new sponge was needed. Meister Mudh informed Alex that a new sponge was quite difficult, if not impossible, to obtain. Instead of using a new sponge, Alex found two old pieces of sponge and inserted them. With his help, the machine functioned normally again.

Also in this area of the factory, Alex found that one or two of the Polish workers often disappeared into a closet and slept while the Germans weren't paying attention or went out somewhere. Alex noticed that they didn't return for several hours. The workers took turns sleeping, and the Germans didn't know they were missing. Alex remembered this when he was very tired and sometimes went into the closet to sleep for several hours.

Alex occasionally walked by the Polish camp outside the factory. He never attempted to go inside the barracks. However, late one evening in the month of May, he was ordered to repair something near the Polish barracks. On his way past the barracks, he saw two German foremen with rubber clubs in their hands near the entrance. As a rule, the Poles had to be in their barracks by 6:00 p.m. One Polish worker was late this day. As he tried to enter his barrack, a German foreman hit him over the head.

Alex learned to read and speak German very well and the Germans recognized him as a very good worker. Additionally, within one and a half months, the Germans became pleased with his cooperative spirit. Meister Mudh and two of the other Germans Alex worked with were Fascists. Even these people liked Alex because they couldn't find anything that would turn them against him.

Occasionally, Meister Mudh would bring Alex one or two sandwiches. He claimed that because Alex worked well, he would have to eat well.

The day's work at the factory was very long. Alex remarked, "The factory workers woke up at 4 a.m., began work at 6 a.m., rested during two 15-minute breaks, and stopped working at 5 p.m."[2] On top of these long hours, the laborers were expected to work additional hours as needed. Workers' rights in the factories were nonexistent.[3]

One time Meister Mudh came to Alex and said, "Alex, I just don't understand. You should be in the German army fighting the

Bolsheviks." Alex replied, "Meister Mudh, French people don't make good soldiers. When we fight, we always lose. Look what happened and how long it took the Germans to take France, two or three weeks? We don't make good soldiers." Later Alex thought to himself, "Why don't you go, Meister Mudh? You're only 33 or 34, and strong." But Alex decided it was better to be silent, so he didn't ask. From that time on, Meister Mudh didn't speak to Alex any more about the German Army.

In late February 1942, Alex decided to leave the school and the Flemish families with whom he stayed in Room #14 in Bremen and went to live in town at the residence of a German family named Tolz. Alex had become friends with Mrs. Tolz, who worked in the cafeteria in the school. Occasionally Alex would come and ask her for more soup and a little extra bread. She would tell him to come back later, and this served him the extra helpings of soup and bread. Mrs. Tolz's husband was a driver who operated the electric car on the street. Her son was a Fascist. She always cautioned Alex, "When my son comes home, don't say anything to him because he's a Fascist. He's being trained in one of the Nazi youth organizations, Hitler Grigeud."

Since he lived in a private home, Alex could go wherever he wanted at night as long as he was punctual at work. Alex said, "I was never late. I never missed a day. I was never sick. I came down with aluminum poisoning only once. But they had an excellent doctor who treated the infection. After three days of rest at home, I was back on the job." Doctor Schmidt gave Alex an injection that completely froze his leg, making it very cold. The injection killed the infection and removed all the pus. The doctor bandaged Alex's leg. Alex felt better after the second day and returned to work.

By March 1942, the Germans had advanced many hundreds of kilometers into Russia. Each day Meister Mudh would pull out his big map of Europe and mark the Nazi advances with a thumbtack. Usually the Germans advanced 50 or 100 kilometers each day. Daily, Meister Mudh was overjoyed with this news.

In April 1942, after Alex had been at the factory for four months, the factory began to be bombed with greater frequency. One part of the factory was leveled during a bombing raid, but the Germans quickly rebuilt it. Much of the factory property was also damaged.

While working at the factory, Alex became good friends with the Ukrainian worker, Hawrilo. Alex knew that Hawrilo didn't like the Germans very much, though Hawrilo never told anyone. Cautiously suspicious of everyone, Alex thought that Hawrilo might not like the Jewish people either so he didn't speak very much to him about the Jews.

In May 1942, Hawrilo was repeatedly told by one of the Fascists to do something. Each time after the job was completed, Hawrilo was told that he did it wrong. The Fascist began to grow hysterical, cursing and swearing violently. Hawrilo, in turn, argued with him. The argument between the two grew increasingly more violent. Finally, the Fascist took a hammer and swung his arms in the air, preparing to hit Hawrilo over the head. At that moment, Alex swiftly went to Hawrilo's aid. Alex was only 2 or 3 meters away and saw that Hawrilo, who was very weak and small, could have been killed. He lunged toward the hammer, and seized it from the Fascist. Alex then said, "Aw, leave him alone. Hawrilo's stupid." The Fascist again looked at Hawrilo and swung at him so angrily that Hawrilo went reeling backward, falling to the ground. Then the German went outside to cool off.

Alex had got along well with all the Germans, so they didn't do anything to him when he seized the hammer. However, after this violent argument, it became increasingly bad for Hawrilo. Hawrilo

71

told Alex, "You saved my life, but they'll still kill me." Alex remarked, "Don't speak or say anything to them. Just do your work. Don't respond with even one word when they talk to you. That's the best and only way."

In time, Hawrilo made a plan. He realized he had to be either sick or dead to not work at the factory. Alex saw that Hawrilo was missing from work for about a week. After inquiring about his whereabouts, Alex was told that Hawrilo had appendicitis and was in the hospital for a checkup. After Alex discovered which hospital Hawrilo was in, he went down to see him. At that time, Hawrilo told Alex, "I'm very sick, Alex. I have to go home." Two or three weeks later, Alex was planning to visit Hawrilo again, but Hawrilo strode into the factory. After taking his work clothes and other belongings, Hawrilo approached Alex and said, "You know Alex, you won't believe this, but they gave me permission to go home." The next day around 7 a.m., Hawrilo and Alex stopped for breakfast. After they had eaten, Alex accompanied Hawrilo to the train, which was to take him back home to the Soviet Union. Alex told him that he didn't like to see him go. Furthermore, Alex told Hawrilo that he was a Jew.

Overwhelmingly surprised by this revelation, Hawrilo declared, "I never could have imagined that you were Jewish. I was convinced that you were a Frenchman." After Alex told his secret, he requested a favor of Hawrilo. "When you reach Poland, could you please write a letter to my parents? I'm very concerned about them and their welfare." Alex gave Hawrilo his family's address in Stary Soncz.

XI

news about stary soncz

Four or five weeks later, Alex received his long awaited reply from Hawrilo. "It's very difficult for me to write this news to you, but your whole family is no longer at the address you gave me," Hawrilo wrote. "The Germans came and captured your family and took them somewhere, and no one knows their whereabouts. They took your mother, your father, and your three sisters. No one in the town of Stary Soncz knows where they are. They certainly no longer live at the address you gave me. Alex, it is not quite like you told me here. Most people are living in the forest. The underground operates out of the forest. It's very difficult for the people in the town, because the German Army has seized all the animals, the cows, the chickens, the hogs, and so forth. Many people are starving to death."

When the Germans first came to Stary Soncz, they forced the Jews to repair roads and other damage from the war. Additionally, they forced Jews to wear some form of identification to label them as Jewish.[1]

The end of 1939 established the Yudenrat.[2] As elsewhere in Poland, every community needed to have a Yudenrat, a Jewish council that functioned to carry out the Germans' orders. A standard requirement of the council was to maintain a census of the Jewish population.[3] For their labor needs, the Germans wanted to know each community's statistics by age and occupation.[4] Every day, the Jews were forced to provide laborers for the Germans' needs, varying from road repair to agricultural work.[5]

The Yudenrat was also responsible for functions normally assigned to a municipality, such as housing, food and water. The Yudenrat supported the Jews, helping the hungry and the sick.[6] Even before the Yudenrat was established, the Jews of Stary Soncz had organized to help each other. In 1937, the community's Jewish merchants had established a fund enabling them to make 135 loans amounting to 19,675 zloty. Based on the (November 2001) exchange rate of 4.1 zloty to the US, this was equivalent to $ 4,700.[7]

For additional supplies, the Yudenrat sought assistance from ZSS, also known as Zydowska Samopomoc Spoleczna, a Jewish communal self-help organization. ZSS was accredited under the government's Department of the Interior and networked with the Red Cross and foreign organizations for money and supplies.[8] The ZSS from Krakow helped 85 Jews, although the Yudenrat reported that 230 Jews needed immediate help.[9]

By 1940, the Germans began to send Jews to labor camps on the grounds that they weren't obeying their restrictions for movement and identification.[10] The Nazi SS, who already had a reputation of terror and violence, operated these labor camps. The workers were insufficiently clothed and fed and forced to work long hours. Some had to walk long distances to get to their place of work. It was common for workers to be beaten and / or killed. Those who tried to escape faced certain death.[11] To avoid being sent to labor camps,

Jews looked for stable jobs. They tried to work where they were needed. Those who worked in vital positions received certificates protecting them from deportation to a labor camp.[12]

In France, Jews also found protection when employed by factories making products for Germany.[13] In September 1942 there were 22 major factories that offered employment and protection. The fur industry hired most of these Jewish workers. By the beginning of 1943, approximately 3,000 Jews held such positions with protection papers.[14]

However, later that year, this protection became less dependable. After being defeated at Stalingrad, Germany no longer needed a large supply of fur products because the winter campaign had ended.[15] Tragically, the heroic example of the German businessman Oskar Schindler was an exception. When other factories stopped employing Jews, he continued to employ Jews in Poland to protect them from death.[16]

In 1942 the Germans established a ghetto, containing 1,000 people, for the Jews of Stary Soncz and the surrounding villages. Due to overcrowding, the ghetto had very bad sanitary conditions, resulting in epidemics. By July 1942, tens of people had died.

On August 17, 1942, the Germans closed the Stary Soncz ghetto, forcing the Jews to walk to Nowy Soncz's ghetto, 9 kilometers away. The Germans killed those who were old or sick and couldn't manage the distance. According to one account, the Germans killed 95 Jews in the forest; according to another account, they killed 150. From Nowy Soncz, the Jews were sent to a concentration camp in Beltz, except for 40 young people who were sent to a working camp instead.[17]

In the year 2000, it became widely known that the Germans were not solely responsible for the atrocities in Poland. There were cases where the Polish people themselves were responsible. One example is the Jedwabne massacre of July 10, 1941 where 1,600 Jews were locked in a barn and burned by their neighbors and residents of neighboring villages.[18] Jedwabne was a village of 2,500 residents, of whom 60 percent were Jewish.[19]

XII

relaxation and transfers

N ot knowing where his parents and sisters were living or even whether they were alive, Alex continued with his life. In the summer of 1942, he occasionally met a Polish girl on Sunday afternoons. They met in the park after work, as did two other Polish workers and their girlfriends. The girls were all very beautiful. Together, they ate food and made music. Alex brought a banjo he had learned to play, and one of the other Polish workers brought a mandolin. One of the girls was an excellent singer. The six of them enjoyed their weekends together.

The following December, Alex took his first five-day vacation. He traveled to France. Upon reaching Paris, he found a strikingly different city from the one he had known. His old city had been turned into a war zone. War rations had affected everyone, rich and poor alike. To keep warm, people were searching the outdoors for leaves, branches, or anything else that would burn. Those people whose homes lacked chimneys used makeshift devices such as old tins and flowerpots and evacuated the smoke through pipes from their kitchen windows. Consequently, apartment fronts became stained with soot.[1]

While Alex was in Germany, the situation had worsened for the Jews in France. In March 1942, the Germans began deporting Jews to Eastern Europe. The following July, deportations dramatically increased.[2] Furthermore, there was another big change. Until July 1942, only men were arrested, most of them immigrants. However, on July 16, 1942, a large number of men, women, and children were hastily arrested by French police. This massive arrest was referred to as "La Grande Rafle." Planned by the Germans but carried out by the French, the authorities hoped to arrest 28,000 prisoners. Despite the planning, 15,884 Jews were arrested over a two-day period. The difference was attributed to the sympathy of Frenchmen making the arrests.[3]

Within the next few weeks, Jewish immigrants began to flee from Paris, seeking refuge in the Vichy Zone, known for not deporting anyone. Internment was a possibility but could be avoided with money.[4]

In 1942, Pastor Andre Trocme became known for rescuing Jews in the village of Le Chambon sur Lignon in southeastern France. With the help of his congregation, he is said to have helped as many as 5,000 Jews.[5] By 1943, with a dwindling supply of foreign Jews, the Germans began deporting French Jews as well in order to meet their deportation schedule.[6]

Alex took his second vacation to Paris three months later in March 1943. After another three months, around late June, Alex spent a third vacation in France. Each time he had special permission from the German officers. Indeed, he was extremely lucky. Each time he came back to Paris, he saw radical changes. On returning from his vacations, Alex would bring back perfume, stockings, and other gifts for his foreman, Meister Mudh, and the other two Fascists. The Germans liked Alex very much because of his consideration and thoughtfulness.

In September 1942, after Alex had worked for nine months at Bremenburg, he received transfer orders. Meister Mudh called Alex and said, "You are to be transferred to the main factory in Bremen. They need you badly." At the Bremen factory, Alex had to hold down two different jobs, one of which was on the assembly line for the mass production of stukas. He was sent to a big hall where all the people were working in a line. Alex commented, "The first time I entered this factory, the noise was so terrific it forced me back outside. It was a drastic change for me." He lived daily with these noisy conditions.

Inside the factory, the riveters assembled the planes. Alex was soon busy using the air hammer to insert the rivets. He also drilled the holes in which the rivets were to be inserted. Alex's position in the line was about the third stage from the beginning, where they were just beginning to assemble the planes. Alex worked on the part between the fuselages.

Alex liked this job better than his job at the first factory. One reason was that he could sleep 20 minutes longer. Another reason was that he had a very good foreman named Hans. Hans was not a Fascist, and he didn't care much for Hitler. However, he was never concerned about his workers either. His only concern was to reach the necessary production output and to get the job done on time. For Alex, this was a more important job than his previous one. The war production output needs were greater and they needed skilled people.

Alex was to remain at this plant from September 1942 until November 1943. Although he liked this job more than the previous one, he disliked many aspects. In addition to the noise level, he found it routine and monotonous. He claimed, "It was a very easy job for stupid people. Everything was automatic." Yet, his job wasn't completely boring. He enjoyed working in a factory where there were many people from different ethnic origins working peacefully and cooperatively together. There were Russians, Italians, Poles, Dutch, Belgians, French, Bulgarians, Romanians, and Yugoslavs. Consequently, he made friends with people of many different nationalities.

One night after getting off from work, Alex received a letter from the Bremen police ordering him to report to the office the next day at 9:00 a.m. He was very frightened and asked one of the Flemish people, who knew and interpreted German better than he did, to go with him. When Alex arrived at the office, there were at least 15 to 20 police officers inside. Alex recalled, "I turned so white, I felt like I didn't have any more blood remaining in me, and I could hear my heart pounding. Yet I was still able to look them straight in the eye." Alex spoke first, "You called me today; what is the problem?"

A policeman who sat by the first desk said, "There's not much of a problem. We just want to know where you are working." Alex answered, "I work at Algemieine Wesser Flugzaigbau in Bremen." He was then asked, "Is your name Alexander Rosenfeld?" Alex replied, "Yes." The interrogation continued. "Did you come from France?" "Yes, I did," he told the policeman. "Do you live at this address?" "Yes," Alex replied. Then the officer pondered and muttered repeatedly, "Rosenfeld... Rosenfeld..." At that point, another policeman at the side and to the rear of the room said, "Yes, there are many Frenchmen who have German names." The first policeman continued to ask questions: "Alex, where are your parents from?"

Alex responded, "I believe my parents came from Alsace Lorraine."

Then they told Alex, "Alright, you can go now." Alex hid his relief and made his way out of the police office. All this time, the Flemish man who accompanied Alex had to remain outside the police office. After he saw Alex, he asked him, "What happened?" Alex remarked, "Why?" He answered, "Because you look like a ghost."

XIII

maria

Alex worked with seven other people in his section of the factory, including Hans, the foreman. There were one Frenchman, two Russian girls named Paula and Maria, a Russian boy, one Dutchman and one Belgian. The Russian boy, Misha, was very young, about 12 years old. He was a very good worker because he was very obedient and quick. Paula was very pretty and not more than 14 or 15 years old. Maria was the oldest, about 16. She was a big girl, not pretty but with a sweet personality. She had pockmarks on her face, which detracted from her appearance.

While his group worked, Alex noticed that the Russians were hardly ever fed. They never had bread and were hungry most of the time. When the Russian girls and boy didn't receive food, they cut grass, put it in hot water, and made soup. Every day Alex would find them hungry. Alex and his work group realized that the Germans were intense in their starvation methods. Slave labor was one method that the Nazis used for extermination.[1] Thus foreign prisoners were treated differently from foreign civilians.

Alex's group organized a way to obtain bread for the Russians. They provided them with bread or whatever food they could save so that the Russians would not go hungry. Other than the Russian girls and boy, the Russian prisoners didn't work directly with Alex. They worked in the next building where they made aluminum for planes and cigarette lighters. When the Germans weren't looking, the Russian prisoners made little 15-centimeter model lighters for any Frenchman who was willing to sell them. The French often sold them to German civilians for bread and other food. Alex noticed that one of the prisoners always had cigarettes. How he got them, no one knew.

One morning Alex went to the factory, taking his drill and hammer, and prepared for work. One minute later, Paula and the young Russian boy Misha came running to Alex and said, "Alex, do you know what happened last night? They're going to kill Maria." Alex asked, "Why?" They said, "Maria worked with us yesterday. When it was time to finish work, she went home with the first group instead of the second group like she was supposed to. There were three work shifts. It wasn't very important because we'd finished our work, but the Germans took Maria and put her in prison. She hasn't eaten since lunchtime yesterday." Alex answered, "Maria will soon be back here working with us. I can't work without her." Then Alex and the others started working.

While Alex made the rivets, he needed someone to hold the steel pieces. This was Maria's job. To take Maria's place, Alex had Paula hold the pieces of steel. Even though Paula wasn't as strong as Maria, she was still able to hold the pieces well. However, in an effort to have Maria returned, Alex intentionally made each rivet wrong (i.e., too flat). Hans came over, stopped the work,

83

and asked, "Why is there a lull in production here?" Alex answered, "I can't work like this. The rivets are all bad; the steel is not being held right." Hans replied, "I'll give you somebody else." Alex remarked, "I want Maria because she knows how to hold the steel." Instead, they gave Alex the young Russian boy, Misha. Again, Alex intentionally made the same mistakes by repeatedly "damaging" several rivets.

The construction of a stuka plane was very important (one defective rivet could destroy the plane). Ten minutes later, Hans stopped the work again and said, "What's the matter with you today, Alex?" Alex replied, "This boy isn't strong enough to hold the steel. I can't work like this. All the rivets are bad. Give me Maria." Two hours passed while Alex continued to make intentional mistakes. Still, Maria had not returned. Then Alex said, "I won't work anymore. I'll be killed if I make a defective plane." Hans argued with Alex for two hours and, fortunately for Alex, Hans saw that the production had come to a standstill.

Hans went to the police office, saying, "We need Maria." One hour later, about 11:30 a.m., Maria came stumbling into the factory. She was in immense pain. She was having spasms after not having eaten for 24 hours. She had been left all night sitting in the dark, in freezing cold. Alex told Maria, "Go under the planes so no one can see you." She cried continuously. Alex told her, "Don't cry, Maria!" Alex sent a Frenchman to bring bread and something else for Maria to eat. Within minutes, he returned with food. Alex gave Maria the food while she continued to hide underneath the planes. He again told her to be quiet and not cry. All the French, Belgian, and Dutch workers eventually brought Maria something to eat.

Meanwhile, Alex had Paula hold the iron for about one half hour until Maria got some nourishment and was feeling well again. The Germans didn't know someone was under the plane. When

Maria finished eating, Alex and Maria began to work together again. He told Maria, "Don't leave early again. Don't look for any more trouble." She thanked Alex for saving her life.

XIV

bombing raids

While working a night shift, Alex met a Frenchman, Nicholas, between the ages of 40 and 45, who had an 18-year old son, Jacque. Jacque worked with metal in the factory and had a nose with a typical Jewish profile. On one occasion Jacques' father started to speak Hebrew to Alex but Alex told him, "I don't know Jewish." In spite of Jacques' nose, Alex didn't want to take chances. He was suspicious of everyone. Nevertheless, Alex became good friends with Nicholas.

Through their conversations, Alex learned that Nicholas and Jacque came from Bordeaux. Nicholas was a barber, and made good money in Germany cutting the hair of many workers. For each haircut, Nicholas received one mark. In one night, he used to earn at least 12 marks. Nicholas and Jacque told Alex that when they leave for France on vacation, they wouldn't return to the factory in Germany. Again, they tried to speak Hebrew to Alex, and again Alex told them that he didn't speak or know Jewish.

He said, "You have to speak French with me." Alex explained his cautiousness later: "Whenever people became friendly with me, no matter who they were, the more frightened and cautious I became. In France I saw too many horrible things happen to the Jewish people."

One time, the Germans sent Alex to work in another area of the factory. He was grouped with three Germans, two Dutch people, and two Frenchmen. While he was working, one of the Germans, Kurt, claimed that Alex was a Jew. "Aw, you must be Jewish," he said. Alex replied, "Why? I'm not Jewish." Kurt replied, "I'm sure you're Jewish." Alex asked, "How are you sure?" "With a name like Rosenfeld you would have to undress for me to be sure," answered Kurt. Alex began to unfasten the belt on his trousers and told him, "Okay, I'll undress and prove to you," and he began to do just that.

As he began to lower his trousers, Kurt remarked, "Forget it, Alex. I was only kidding you. It's not necessary. I believe you." Constantly flashing through Alex's mind was the thought that he could be found out one day.

Alex had strong memories of the Allied planes' bombing raids. He recalled of one night, "When I lived in the Tolz's home, I was looking out the window when I saw all of Bremen on fire. Everywhere I looked, the whole city was aflame. I thought of what Rome might have looked like in the days of Nero." Two or three weeks later, special phosphor bombs fell on Hamburg. Several times later the Allies dropped these bombs on Bremen. One such bomb fell about 230 meters from Alex's barracks. Fortunately, it didn't come into the barracks. Many people were wounded very badly with first-degree burns.

The Germans were very good firefighters and had excellent fire- fighting equipment. They also had special rubber, fire-resistant clothing and special material with which they put out the fires. As a rule, only the special rubber clothes could protect anyone from the phosphor fires.Most of the phosphor bombs were dropped on Hamburg. For two straight days and two straight nights, Alex could see Hamburg burning and aflame. Although Hamburg was some 130 kilometers away from Bremen, the bright, shiny red sky above Hamburg was clearly visible. Two Frenchmen later informed Alex that they had come from Hamburg, where many people were "burning alive" in the streets and buildings.

During a bombing raid, the factory alarms sounded and people were quickly ordered to leave their posts and go to the bunkers. This hindered the Germans from having someone watch the factory. After the bombings, people had to put sand or water on the fires depending on the type of bombs.

One day, the Germans requested that someone sleep in the factory. As a reward they offered three marks per night and good soup in the evening. Alex was very interested in the offer of three marks. It was the equivalent of two hours work for him, and he didn't care whether he slept at home or in the factory.

Alex commenced sleeping in the factory each night, and there he met many Belgian, Flemish, Dutch, and French friends. The workers in the factory all had armbands signifying whether they were French, Dutch, Belgian, Italian, Bulgarian, and so forth. Alex had the French band but half of the time he didn't put it on. Once a German came and asked Alex, "Where's your arm band?" Alex responded, "Oh, in my pocket, I forgot to put it on." The German ordered Alex to put it on, which he did. Five minutes later, after the German was gone, Alex removed it.

At night, Alex would talk with the Dutch people, many of whom became his good friends. The Germans weren't in charge at night. Instead, some of the workers, including one Dutchman named Van Burke, took over the responsibilities.

Alex could never sleep peacefully in the factory, even for one night. Every two, three or four hours, the Allied planes came and attempted to bomb the factory, but the bombs didn't always fall on target. Bremen suffered extensive damage. Alex remembered that on one occasion there were probably 1,000 planes that flew over the city. They were exceptionally high in the sky and made a terrible noise. Bremen was destroyed in this mass incendiary bombing raid. Alex remarked, "In every two or three houses on the street, the Germans had anti-aircraft batteries. There were 6 or 8 people to each anti-aircraft battery. Not only did I hear the bombs fall from the sky, but the reply of the anti-aircraft guns also made a terrible noise. The entire city of Bremen and all the homes shook and vibrated from the noise. There was much destruction." Alex further remarked about this attack, "But for me, it was nothing. I wasn't scared or frightened. I was only concerned that a piece of one of the fragmentary bombs might hit me." Such fragments in hands, legs, etc., had wounded many of his friends when they went outside. Often, people didn't have enough time to get to the shelter areas.

During bombing attacks, Alex never tried to go to the bunker or shelter. He knew that when the bombs came he would be as dead in the bunkers as in the factory. Instead, he felt he had a greater chance of escaping death by standing near a door in the building.

However, when the German police came, Alex had to go inside the bunker with all the elderly people, children, and workers.

By 1943, Allied planes had intensified their aerial raids and bombings. United States military planes bombed German cities in the daytime and the British Royal Air Force bombed the cities at night.[1] These bombing raids occurred up to five or six times each night. Sometimes, though rarely, half a day would go by without any bombing, but the raids resumed soon after. Every day they bombed, without exception. Occasionally, the planes would pass on their way to Berlin, but the alert was still on. Work was still halted.

In the early winter of 1943, Alex was working during the night shift. It was approximately 10:00 p.m. when one Frenchman came running inside to him. "Alex, Alex, come and see something extraordinary outside." Alex ran outside and saw a lot of people standing looking skyward. There in the sky was a beautiful rainbow, which spread across the horizon from east to west. It lasted for about 20 minutes. It was the first time in his life that Alex had seen such a beautiful rainbow.

No one knew how this rainbow was possible and no one was able to offer an explanation. Some workers interpreted it as the beginning of the end for the Nazis. Others interpreted it as the bridge between the Americans and British from the west and the Russians from the east. It was mostly the French people who offered these interpretations. When the Germans were asked the meaning of the rainbow, they remarked that they didn't know, or explained that the Nazis had made an artificial rainbow.

XV

production problems,
planned and unplanned

One day in June 1943, Alex was working the night shift in an area where most of the workers were French prisoners making the fuselage. Alex and the others were having much trouble with their work. Alex had to drill holes for the rivets, but each time he drilled there were two holes too many. He asked the workers, "Why is this happening?" But no one knew.

The foreman started screaming, "Why are there too many holes?" Investigators were called in to try to detect the cause of the extra holes. Alex was frightened and anxious to know the cause, because he thought the Germans might accuse him of sabotage. Seven inspectors spent all day studying the specification forms that the workers had been using before they figured out the problem. They changed the specification and from that time it was all right. It had been a big problem for Alex and for the Germans. The problem was traced to a German construction engineer who had made the specification.

By mid-summer, Alex and others in the factory had become active in creating production problems. However, they had to be careful, because there was constant surveillance. Germans patrolled the factories at all times. The Germans gave their workers orders not to leave the factory with even one piece of Plexiglas, as the material was very expensive. Alex made many "beautiful little stukas" from the Plexiglas. He badly wanted to take one stuka from the factory but couldn't do so.

The Germans at the gate were very strict. They always checked the workers' bags as they left at the end of their day's work. Alex devised a plan. One day as he prepared to leave the factory, he approached one of the policemen and said, "You know, I'd like to make you something in my spare time, something beautiful." "All right," said the guard. Alex asked him, "How about a little stuka from plexiglas?" The policeman replied, "Okay." Alex then explained, "But it would have to be on one condition. I'll make one for you, provided that I can make one for myself."

A few days later, Alex brought the policeman his stuka. In time, due to this policeman's continual trust, he stopped checking Alex's baggage or belongings at the close of each workday as he did with the other workers. Consequently, Alex was able to take home almost 100 little stukas. Alex sold these stukas in the street for 100 marks each. Ironically, one German told Alex, "You French people are funny people. We can put you all in one prison, naked, starving, and completely isolated, and after two hours you'll have clothes and food. How you accomplish this, I can't comprehend or understand."

By late summer, the Frenchmen were thoroughly organized with their sabotage efforts. The workers in the factory were ordered, "Every night before going to your bedroom, put one or two pounds of rivets in your pockets and hide them in your bedroom."

When the workers went back to work, they would have to make new rivets. All the Frenchmen complied with this order. There must have been 300 to 400 rivets being taken into the workers' bedrooms each night.

The Frenchmen who worked with the rivets also tried to spoil them as much as possible. The result was a severe shortage of rivets. This played havoc with the German supervisors. Toward the end, the German foremen became scared because they couldn't keep up with the war production quota. The workers realized that the more they sabotaged, the sooner the war would come to an end.

In addition to sabotaging the production of rivets, the workers found other methods. One Belgian knew that three trains would roll into the Bremen station carrying ammunition. The Belgian blew up the three trains. Immediately, the Germans killed the Belgian, but they had lost three trainloads of munitions.

A friend of Alex's reported another event to him. One set of barracks held Czech prisoners. The Czechs started to strike and make demonstrations. They refused to work. The Germans rounded them up and shot or massacred all 300 of the Czechs. Then they burned the Czechs' clothes and barracks.

Another method of sabotage was helping the Allied bombers locate their targets. At 10:30 or 11:00 p.m. one night in August 1943, several Allied planes were in the sky while Alex was in the factory. He was working with 10 to 15 French prisoners, several Dutch, and 4 or 5 Germans. They all heard the air raid signal. The German foreman commanded them, "Don't go to the bunkers. Stay and work." All the people continued to work. The Frenchmen said, "We don't want to be killed. We must go to the bunkers." The German foreman said, "No." But, while the Frenchmen stayed, the Germans went to the bunker.

After the Frenchmen heard the planes and then the German

anti-aircraft batteries, they opened the large doors to the factory. Five took one side and five took the other side. The pilots in the sky immediately spotted the great light on the ground. One half of the lit factory could be seen. Less than minutes later, the prisoners all ran hurriedly to the bunker. The Allied planes were then able to make a direct hit. So many bombs fell in the area that the factory was fatally damaged.

XVI

special friendships

While Alex lived at the Tolz's home, he became very friendly with a beautiful 22-year-old German blonde whose name was Hilda. He first met her at a picturesque park about 300 meters from his house. He recalled one day when he was sitting in the park's garden: "Hilda approached and sat on one of the nearby benches. I had never seen such a beautiful young woman before." Each day she would come to the garden to sit. She looked at Alex. Alex, in turn, glanced at her. They sat for 10 or 15 minutes. One day she asked Alex questions and he answered her. He told her he was a Frenchman who worked at the Stuka factory in Bremen. He also told her that he was merely resting in the garden. She said, "I'd like to speak with you again. You know that we're not allowed to speak with strangers or be with strangers here. But when it gets dark, I'd like to meet you here. At 9 p.m. tonight we'll go together." Unlike Alex's previous friendship with the Polish woman, this one had to be secretive.

Due to the intensified bombing raids, German security measures had become stricter. At 9 p.m. that evening, Alex and Hilda began their courtship. Alex saw her for about six months, usually two or three nights a week. After courting for a while, Hilda told Alex to come to her house at night instead of meeting in the park. Hilda was married. Since her husband worked at a factory about 500 kilometers from Bremen, she was left alone except that her young sister lived with her. Alex frequented her house all the time. Hilda was very good to Alex because she liked him very much. When Alex didn't go to see her for one reason or another, she would bring food to him in the factory. Toward the end, she was even willing to go to France with him. She said, "When you go to France, Alex, take me. I want to go with you."

Alex was very lucky that his involvement with Hilda didn't lead to trouble. Another Frenchman who worked in Alex's factory was less fortunate. He was a war prisoner, an engineer by trade and highly skilled. Because of his skills, the Germans reassigned him to an office. In time, he fell in love with a German girl who worked at the same office. They made a rendezvous together. One of the German girl's friends felt something wasn't right and reported it to the police. The Frenchman and the German girl were both arrested. When they tried to escape, the Germans killed the Frenchman and sent the girl to a concentration camp. No one ever heard from the girl or learned what was her fate.

In September 1943, a German policeman came to the Tolz's home. He delivered an order from the German Government stating that no strangers could any longer reside in private homes. All strangers had to live in barracks. Along with many others, Alex went back to live in the barracks. In Alex's barracks, there were several Frenchmen in one room, and Dutch in the next. All these strangers lived together harmoniously.

Also in that September it became difficult to get bread. As in France, food was not rationed fairly. Alex was able to find several French workers who were skilled at creating fake bread tickets. This enabled them to obtain greater quantities of bread.

The Germans gave preferential treatment to athletic people who agreed to participate in their recreational programs. Through a bulletin, they advertised their offer: "If anyone will participate in athletic activities, he will receive two more pounds of bread."

Alex promptly joined the sports organization in the barracks. One of the French had practiced ju-jitsu for seven years. He was very strong and Alex was slightly afraid of him. However, Alex said he would try to fight him. Alex remembered how they fought together outside on a beautiful Sunday afternoon. Even though the Frenchman was an expert, Alex defeated him. From that time on, Alex was recognized as the best athlete.

There was also a boxer, Chocke, who lived in Alex's barracks. He was about 6'2" and the Belgian Champion. After he saw Alex defeat the ju-jitsu Frenchman, Chocke motioned Alex over and said, "I'm going to teach you how to box." "I'll try," Alex replied. In spite of his 27 years of age, Alex learned very quickly and Chocke trained him in record time. Alex defeated several people and became well respected as an athlete by all the Frenchmen.

In October, there was a huge sports exhibition. Chocke was challenged to combat two German boxers from Bremen who were both soldiers. Chocke knocked both men out in less than two minutes each. At a later date, Chocke got spray paint in his eyes while he was working and almost lost one of his eyes. The Germans eventually permitted him to return to Belgium.

XVII

bombing intensified

By the end of October 1943, the Allies' bombs continued to cause fatal damage to the Bremen factory. Alex remembered the fear of a young 19-year-old Frenchman. The Germans had just brought him to the barracks. On his first night, there was a strong alarm and bombs started falling. The young Frenchman became hysterical. He was so frightened that the other workers held him. They told him, "Whether you're scared or not, being scared won't help you. Just take the necessary precautions."

The workers had already lived through it for two years. After two days, the young Frenchman had become as white as a sheet. It was hard for most people at the factory to believe, but the 19 year-old already had white and gray hair. Alex commented, "I never saw anyone more frightened than him in my life." All in all, in spite of the danger, the prisoners and workers were glad that more bombs were falling because, as Alex put it, "The more bombs that come, the sooner the war will end."

Through all this turmoil, Alex never missed one day of work, except for the brief time when he had aluminum poisoning. The Germans rewarded Alex by giving him an aluminum plaque with stukas called the "Tuchtig arbeiter," a distinction for being an outstanding worker. Alex always carried this plaque in his suitcase. The plaque would later help him get back safely to France.

By November, the Allies had almost completely bombed out the stuka factory. Consequently, production went very slowly. Most of the machines worked very sluggishly. In spite of the many bombings, Alex always escaped unharmed.

On one of Alex's last nights at the factory, he was in his barracks when the alarms sounded. One minute later he heard the noise of a thousand planes. The houses shook from the vibrations. The anti-aircraft opened fire. Bombs fell into the barracks and one of Alex's Dutch friends lost his leg. Alex didn't go to the bunker but stayed where he was. When he looked outside and saw a bomb begin to burn one foot away from the barracks, he hurriedly jumped through the window. He dropped sand on the burning bomb.

When he returned, one Frenchman yelled at him, "Alex, are you crazy? Why'd you take a chance like that with a bomb?" Alex replied, "It's nothing. I only wanted to save the barracks and my suitcase and belongings."

After the principal factory was completely destroyed and all the machines were demolished, Alex received a notice to report to the police office. A German officer told Alex, "You have here your money and your papers; you are assigned to be transferred to the Algiers factory in Uhingen." In late November 1943, Alex took his belongings and boarded the train to Uhingen. Uhingen was located some 37 kilometers south of Stuttgart in the southern part of Germany. The train trip took close to two days and two nights. The train was seldom on schedule.

At the Algiers factory, there were big presses for manufacturing tanks. Alex made the form only, working with two or three ton pieces of steel. He was assigned to cut the steel and put two pieces of steel together. Great precision was required. He worked relentlessly for a good foreman. In contrast to the Bremen factory, most of the factory workers were German. The Germans inside the factory again got along well together. A few others were French. Alex was very disappointed with Uhingen, which was a tiny town. The houses, however, were very clean inside and beautiful on the outside. The village also had beautiful gardens and parks.

Alex went to the address where he was to stay in Uhingen and met with the lager furer. Almost immediately, the lager furer and Alex developed an intense dislike for each other. The lager furer was a devoted and almost fanatical Fascist. He looked at Alex in a very peculiar way, and Alex became frightened. Soon after Alex's move, it was time for his vacation. When he came to see the lager furer in the barracks, Alex said, "I've now been two years in Germany and it's time for my vacation."

The lager furer asked, "Do you have your French passport?" Alex replied, "No. I just have my red German passport." The lager furer advised him, "You can't go without your French passport." The lager furer further informed him, "I'll write to the French prefecture (police) in Paris." Alex then told the lager furer, "I'll pick it up in Paris." The lager furer insisted, "You can't go."

From that time on, the German lager furer was very suspicious, and Alex's fears increased to new heights and proportions. He became very apprehensive when he was denied permission to go to France. Alex was convinced that the lager furer was out to make trouble for him.

There were 400 Russian officers confined in Uhingen for the purpose of extermination. Every day, the German soldiers would take nine Russian officers outside to be either hanged or shot. Alex observed, "They never came back. The Germans never liked the Russian officers. They only had them at Uhingen to be killed."

After Alex had worked for about three weeks, the situation with the lager furer worsened. Alex knew he would never get permission for a vacation. He understood that they were going to hold him in Germany. He also knew that a letter would come from the French prefecture, or police, saying that no French passport had been issued to a Frenchman named Rosenfeld. Alex discovered a Frenchman who was about to go to France on a vacation. Alex told him, "I have to go tomorrow." The Frenchman replied, "You can go with us in two or three weeks. My girlfriend will be here, and we can all go together." Alex replied, "You know, if I can have your stamped permission, I'll give you 300 marks. When they ask you what happened to your passport, just tell them you lost it. They'll issue a new one." When the Frenchman asked, "Are you sure the police will give me a new permission?" Alex answered in the affirmative. Since the Frenchman would have to work one month for 300 marks, he agreed and accepted the 300 marks. Alex, in turn, received the passport to France.

XVIII

escape to France

It was an afternoon in November. Alex was very scared. He left all of his clothes and most of his belongings in his barracks. First, he spoke with several French prisoners and said, "When I go back to France, I'm going by way of Strasburg." One Frenchman advised him, "No, you mustn't. They'll catch you for sure. Never go by way of Strasburg. The control is too rigid at Strasburg. Many of our friends were caught there. If you are to escape, then go by way of Milhausen near the Swiss and French frontiers." Before he could leave Uhingen, Alex needed to go to three offices. Hurriedly, he went to the arbeitsamt, the workers' office, then to the travel office to have his passport stamped, and finally to the police office.

At the police office, the police asked him various questions. "Are you a war prisoner?" Alex answered, "No, I volunteered to work in Germany. I've been here now for two years. I have permission for a five-day vacation." Alex asked, "Can I take six days of vacation instead of five? I don't think I'll have enough time to accomplish everything and go to all the places I'd like." They told him, "No, you can't. If you stay one extra day we'll bring you back with force." They then stamped his papers, much to his relief.

Alex went to Stuttgart where he boarded the first train in the evening. He headed for Milhausen where he hoped to cross the frontier. In his suitcase, he had the aluminum plaque that he had received in the Bremen factory. Alex chose to ride second class to be sure he had a place to sit. However, there were a large number of people on the train, and he couldn't find either a second-or a third-class seat. Alex looked for a place in the other cars.

Eventually, in one cabin, he saw an empty seat. Also in the cabin there were two young German officers accompanied by two women and three other civilians. There was only one place left. Not noticing that it was a first class cabin, Alex entered and stopped before one of the young German officers. He asked, "Is this seat taken?" The officer responded, "No, you can sit here." Alex sat down between the two officers. He put his suitcase aside, and in a matter of minutes he fell asleep.

An hour or so later, Alex was aroused from his sleep by some-one patting him on his shoulder. Looking up he could see it was the same German officer he had sat beside. The officer said, "Hey, you're sleeping on my arm." Alex told him, "I'm sorry." Soon after this the conductor came by and asked for his ticket. Alex gave him his ticket, but the conductor advised him that he would have to get off the car because it was first class and he had a second-class ticket. Alex tried unsuccessfully to convince him that he didn't know, and that he was certain it was a first class ticket.

After he left his compartment, he couldn't find another emp-ty space, but the sleep he had received in the first-class compart-ment really helped. He remained in the corridor of the train until they reached Milhausen. It was very early in the morning. The train had traveled all night. The conductor shouted, "Milhausen."

As Alex looked out the window of the train, he could see many soldiers and barbed wire all around. No one could escape very easily. Six or eight soldiers were inspecting all the passengers. When they came to Alex, they asked him his name. He answered the exact name of the Frenchman from whom he had received the permission. When they asked for his papers, he showed them his permission. A German corporal looked at the papers, and a German officer looked inside his suitcase. The officer saw his plaque of distinction, the aluminum plate with the stukas, and he quickly closed the suitcase and said to the corporal, "All Right."

From Milhausen, Alex took the train to Troy and another from Troy to Paris. After he arrived in Paris, he went directly to his former home at 35 Maubert Place. The French superintendent of the building was very happy and surprised to see him, and Alex was likewise glad to see her and find her still alive.

Alex didn't know it at the time, but he had narrowly escaped. Just one or two days after he had crossed out of Germany, the Germans completely closed down the border. No longer were Frenchman allowed at all to return to France from Germany.

In Paris, many of Alex's former acquaintances and friends told him of the terror, murder, and violence everywhere. It was terrible. The Germans had killed thousands of civilians. Food was very scarce. Whatever remote possibility Alex had of returning to Germany had vanished. He could not go back there.

Alex told the French people he met that "Germany is not for me."He informed his superintendent at Maubert Place, "If a letter ever comes for me, just hold on to it for me. If anyone comes personally asking about me, please tell them that you

Above is a pass believed to be given to Alex while in the labor camp in Bremen, Germany which gave permission to go on leave.

haven't seen me. If the Gestapo comes looking for me, tell them I didn't not come here." Alex placed his complete trust in the superintendent.

In Paris, Alex went to Israel and Clara Erdman's apartment to see if he could find his cousins. When he arrived, the apartment was closed. He next went to the superintendent of the building at Maubert Place and asked, "Do you know where Mr. and Mrs. Erdman are?" The superintendent answered, "They went some place, but I don't know where. They vanished a couple of other times, too. The Gestapo came to take them away several times, but no one, including the Erdman's, was inside. Perhaps... Erdman did tell me to tell you to go three houses down from this one. A lady lives there who might know where he is." Alex went to the house down the street where a young French Catholic family lived. They gave Alex the Erdmans' address in southern France. Alex was pleased to find out where the Erdmans might be located. He payed them well for this information. It was not the address of the Erdmans', but the address of his old neighbor.

The address read Mr. and Mrs. Sally, Azay-le-Ferron. Like many other Jews, they had fled to unoccupied France.

Alex had five days to complete all his business. On the second day, he left the French family and the superintendent at Maubert Place. Before he departed, he gave the superintendent one little stuka that was manufactured from the Plexiglas. She told him, "You know, you can join the underground, Alex." He replied, "First, I'd like to see my friends in southern France." He had conclusively decided not to return to Germany, and, at the same time, he knew he couldn't stay in Paris. Everywhere he looked, Alex couldn't find any Jews. It was also impossible to work in Paris, and, without working, he couldn't eat. Food was three times the normal price and he had no ration cards. There was nothing left for him to do in Paris.

XIX

journey to Azay le Feron

Alex took the train headed to Chateauroux in unoccupied France. On the way he encountered another strict paper control point at the train station in Vierzon. The whole train was stopped, closed, and boarded by German soldiers. There were countless German soldiers outside. It was impossible to escape or go from one train to another. Six or eight soldiers leaped onto the train to inspect the occupants and investigate the luggage.

A German officer came to Alex and asked, "Where are you going?" Alex replied, "To Chateauroux." He gave the officer the permission papers he had received from the Uhingen factory and the police. This was enough for the German officer. The Germans inspected his suitcase. Unfortunately, Alex had left his plaque of distinction in Maubert Place. Thankfully, he didn't need it. The Germans approved him for his departure by train.

After Vierzon, Alex wasn't frightened any more. The train started up again, and in time arrived to Chateauroux. Alex remembered, "How good it felt to be free again." The first thing he did when he arrived in Chateauroux, he ate at a French restaurant. He ate veraciously. Of that dinner, he said, "I couldn't remember when I ate so well! It had been such a long time." At the restaurant, Alex obtained directions to Azay le Ferron.

That afternoon, he reached the address of Mr. and Mrs. Sally. Mrs. Sally answered the door. The Sally's had two children, both daughters, one 18 and the other 14. Mrs. Sally was a small woman but still very young and exceedingly pretty for her age. She was neat and industrious. Alex asked her, "Do Mr. and Mrs. Erdman live here?" She replied, "They don't live here." "Do you know where they live?" Alex asked her. Mrs. Sally responded, "Go to the coffee shop; it's possible they might know."

Alex went to the coffee shop, but no one there knew where the Erdmans lived. While Alex was at the coffee shop, Mrs. Sally went to the Erdmans' residence and described the man asking about them. Mrs. Erdman was surprised and exclaimed, "That's my cousin!"

The Erdman's were thrilled and happy to see Alex and he was likewise exceedingly happy and joyful to see them. Alex told them his story of the last two years. Mrs. Erdman, who had lived in Berlin with her husband, said, "Alex, if the Germans didn't take you in those two years, you've just performed a miracle. We just can't understand how you did it. You must have had many chances. We honestly never expected to see you again." The Erdmans then told Alex about the concentration camps and the massacres of the Jews and all the other things that were happening during the war.

Alex asked them how they managed to flee from Paris. They answered, "We paid much money to get through safely. We took the river to the German control point. The Germans watched the river near a bridge." They explained how they walked like real young lovers, arm in arm, past the control point, practically un-noticed. All they had in their possession was a little sack of money. All the Germans did was shake their finger at them, sort of cautioning them to take it slowly-not too much, don't overdo it. The Germans thought they were just out to make love.

Alex then asked Mr. Erdman, "How can I get into the French resistance?" He replied, "This is a little town. I'll take care of it for you. Just don't go outside much. It's safer for you."

Alex's desire to join the resistance was common for young men in France. Instead of going off to perform slave labor for the Germans, many chose the life of a resistance fighter.[1]

Alex was advised by Erdman to wait until 7:30 in the evening, and that a man named Delacroix would come to see him. Delacroix happened to be the postmaster in Azay le Ferron, and he was also the chief of the underground there. The Erdmans didn't tell Alex this at the time. In fact, they told him almost nothing. Mr. Erdman did say, "Whatever Delacroix says to you will be all right." Mr. Delacroix came. The two men briefly exchanged greetings and conversation.

Delacroix told Alex, "I have one farm where I'm going to take you. You can stay at this farm for a week, and then we'll give you directions from there. Someone will come to you with news. Just don't go anywhere. Stay at the farm and work."

This was good news for Alex. It was now snowing and the start of winter. The farm belonged to Mr. and Mrs. Pournin and was situated about five or ten kilometers from Azay le Ferron. There were no houses in the distance; everything was quiet and peaceful. Alex helped out by doing chores. The Pournin's fed Alex as if he were their only child. They also served excellent wine. Two other people worked at the farm, a girl named Madeline and a young Frenchman named Jules, aged 23, who worked with the horses.

Alex worked hard for the first two days, which were bitterly cold. He didn't take the necessary precautions with regards to warm clothing and he became very sick with a stomach cold. The Pournin's found out and called a doctor. The doctor informed Alex, "This isn't bad. You haven't been eating well for the last two years, and you've encountered a great deal of change. Just eat slowly." Alex spent one day in bed, and afterwards he felt better and returned to his farm chores. He worked with Jules, cutting the wood, feeding the animals, and performing other farm work.

In late November a man named Pierre came to see Alex, sent by Delacroix. Pierre was about 24 and was a lieutenant in the French underground. Pierre told Alex, "If anyone comes here to ask you who you are, just say that you work here. Don't say anything else, and in a few days I'll come and take you away from here."

The French resistance evidently checked Alex out and found that he had no affiliation with the Germans and was not a spy. This check took approximately two weeks. Meanwhile, the people at the Pournins' farm, Madeline and Jules, were friendly to Alex. The food was excellent. Alex ate meat two times a day, which was a lot in wartime.

XX

introduction to the French Underground

It was around the middle of December 1943 that Alex left with Lt. Pierre, an excellent officer. Pierre had trained at the Cire, to be reputed to be one of the best military schools in France. Pierre introduced Alex to the underground resistance group in Azay le Ferron. This group was part of the first one formed in the region of Mezier en Brenne. The Mezier group was part of the 17 Chasser a Pied, who went out to hunt and kill the enemy. The members were mostly French soldiers from the French Army. There were no politics involved. The underground was united with one goal: to liberate France from German control.

There were 10 men who reported to the group, including Pierre and Alex. On the second day, 15 to 20 more people came to the camp, including Commandant Carol who was in charge of the resistance. He was the organizer of the underground for Mezier en Brenne, including the entire Indre area. Carol was an older officer, between 50 and 55 years of age. He was tall in stature and had fought with the Africa Legion Etranger.

Prior to the formalized resistance groups, individuals acted separately carrying out various acts of sabotage. Although the Germans tried to eliminate sabotage with public executions, the resistance continued. The resistance groups carried on with the same type of sabotage as the individual acts.[1]

During the first year of German occupation, the resistance movement lacked political leadership. Three separate non-communist groups formed in Lyons, which became the central city of the Resistance Movement. Their differing political views and personalities kept them from unifying. Furthermore, their lack of money, weapons, and experience affected their strength.[2]

After Germany invaded Russia in June 1941, French communists became active in the resistance movement. However, it wasn't until 1942 that the movement became effectively unified under the leadership of Jean Moulin. He convinced the different factions that they needed to be properly supplied with money, guns, and radios from England. To get this assistance, they needed to agree to accept the leadership of Charles de Gaulle, an army officer who had fled to England when the Germans arrived.[3][4]

The separate groups agreed. The British helped organize these groups, who in turn provided England with valuable intelligence. They provided information such as the locations of German airfields or the results of British bombing raids.[5] Within these resistance groups, Jews comprised a disproportionately large percentage.[6] In June 1942, Phillippe Henriot said that the police found Jews responsible for 80% of the Parisian region's attacks upon the German army. Henriot later became the Vichy government's secretary for information and propaganda.[7]

France was not the only country with a resistance movement during World War II. There were resistance movements in every country occupied by the enemy. In Russia, the resistance movement included half a million men and women.[8]

In Paris there were many resistance groups whose functions varied. Some groups helped people cross the border between occupied and unoccupied France. They forged papers and documents that looked identical or very similar to the original German papers.[9]

The need for the Underground's assistance heightened as the Jewish community recognized the increased frequency of the roundups, in addition to the loss of their businesses and the experience of much humiliation from the Nazi racial laws. By train, car, bicycle, and foot, families would travel across the Demarcation Line. With the help of resisters, new homes were found in unoccupied France.[10]

In addition to providing border-crossing assistance within France, the Underground helped with border crossing to other countries. The Underground helped refugees obtain false passports and escape over mountains through Spain to Portugal, a neutral country from which they could obtain visas to travel elsewhere.[11]

Soon after Germany invaded France, the resistance movement received considerable support from a group of Americans who had formed an Emergency Rescue Committee. Their representative, Varian Fry, went to Vichy to help political and intellectual refugees who were individually being hunted by the Germans.[12] With a selectively chosen staff, Fry helped over 1,000 people leave France within an eight-month period.[13]

Alex's group's camp was located 13 kilometers down a dirt road that connected with a main asphalt paved highway. The group was supplied with the equipment they needed, including a large tent for the kitchen. They had a great deal of food in the camp, such as meat, cheese, bread, and eggs. Carol divided their tasks very quickly.

By December 1943, the group had grown to include at least 60 men. They engaged in rigorous physical exercise routines and practiced firing machine guns and rifles and throwing hand grenades, often in the forest. Alex worked relentlessly with an American machine gun. Carol taught the men many different guerrilla tactics. Within the space of one minute, the men had to be able to prepare their belongings and be ready for combat or relocation. Even if they had to be awakened from their sleep, the one-minute requirement applied.

After Alex had been in the underground for two weeks, he received his first orders. He and the other men had to travel at night. All the men had to go, except for a couple who remained behind to watch the camp. The men took four trucks, each carrying 15 men. They had orders that if the Germans blocked the road they were to use force to get through. They knew they had a crucial mission to complete. In case the situation warranted its usage, Alex had one machine gun hidden from view above the area where the chauffeur sat. After several kilometers, the men drove through a little town where the Germans policed the road. The four trucks passed through so swiftly that the German soldiers didn't have sufficient time to close the road. The Germans didn't notice any of the men hidden inside the trucks.

After driving several more kilometers, they came to an open field. Pierre told the men, "We have orders to pick up supplies tonight. A plane will come with ammunition for us. When I give the signal, be prepared to light the fires, to extinguish them, and to run into the field to pick up the supplies."

When the plane arrived on schedule, at midnight, Pierre gave the signal. He lit a little fire, and the other men followed by lighting thirty other fires. The next job was to find where the parachutes carrying the necessary supplies had landed. There were six separate groups for this purpose. Pierre knew how many containers the men needed to look for. They found all the parachutes, took all the supply containers, and set them on the four trucks. Then they went back into the forest to their camp.

Four days later, they accomplished an identical mission. They brought back an abundance of arsenal, dynamite, machine guns, grenades, and transistor radios to hear the latest news. By the end of December 1943, the underground at Azay le Ferron had at their disposal plenty of ammunition for attacks, enough for 200 men. Alex attributed their success to Pierre's guidance. He instructed his men to use different roads when returning from a mission to keep hidden from the Germans.

Pierre was very intelligent, and Alex was able to learn a great deal from him. The officer taught Alex and the other men how to use acid detonators and how to adjust the dynamite for strong explosions and light explosions. He taught the men how much plastic was necessary for the demolition of a bridge, including how long a wire would burn before reaching the detonator. He also trained them how to explode a railroad track with special magnetic bombs set off by an acid detonator. In case the Germans ever confronted one of their trucks with a tank or better artillery, he taught them how to set the magnet to quickly demolish the truck and its contents.

In January 1944, two weeks after the first plane came with ammunition, 24 men received orders to go to a certain roadside and be ready to fight. Older men were also to be ready for combat. That evening they went to the roadside in the forest and set up their machine gun nests. They knew the German Army was to pass nearby. It was very dark. The group spread out and waited for three hours. They were well prepared for this because they had slept during the day. Their orders were to make sure that two machine guns were aimed in the direction of the forthcoming German trucks. The other men in the center were to throw grenades.

After a long silence, two columns of Germans soldiers marched down the country road. There were over 1,000 German soldiers with trucks containing ammunition. The orders were to wait until at least half the German column had passed and the trucks with the ammunition were in range. Suddenly, Pierre gave the signal. The small band instantly opened fire with their weapons and grenades.

The surprised Germans sprang from the trucks. The ammunition trucks in the vicinity all burst into fire and burned brightly. The Germans returned fire, but didn't know where the enemy was because of the pitch black. Everything happened very swiftly. Within two minutes, the orders were to retreat. The resistance retreated without the loss of a single individual.

On many occasions during the daytime, Alex's group used their knowledge of where the Germans were going to pass. They would take dynamite and explode a tree to block the road so the German trucks couldn't pass. It took considerable time and effort for the Germans to clean the roads.

In late January 1944, two Frenchmen from the Azay le Ferron underground were watching for Germans approaching. When the Germans came, the Frenchmen began to open fire with their machine guns. However, their machine guns jammed, and both men were killed. The Frenchmen in the camp were so angered and incensed by this tragic incident that they wanted revenge. Several of them went to town for strong steel wire. They knew the road where the Germans were to pass in the daytime. Furthermore, they had seen Germans speeding by on this road with their motorcycles. Knowing that a motorcyclist couldn't see the wire, they tied the steel wire from tree to tree. Within a short time, two German motorcyclists came by. One hit the wire and fell from his motorcycle.

The second plowed into the first motorcycle while attempting to halt, and also fell from his motorcycle. From their hiding spot in the forest, the Frenchmen came over and killed the Germans. Then they took their guns and fled from the area. Moments later, other German soldiers discovered the two bodies in the roadway.

Alex's membership card for the French Underground in the 17th light infantry under the command of Commandant Carol.

These methods proved to be effective tactics for harassing the Germans. From that time on, it became easy for the Frenchmen to ambush small groups of Germans and kill them. The German soldiers came to be very frightened even when they were with larger groups. When they came into a village or town, their first concern was the underground. They would ask the townspeople, "Do you know if there are any terrorists here in town or in a nearby town?"

The people in the town would merely reply, "We don't know of any terrorists." If anyone helped the Germans, the underground would surely kill the collaborator.

XXI

underground missions

On a beautiful Sunday in March 1944, Pierre told the group that 24 men were to go 40 kilometers away to Blanc. These men traveled to the first small village past Blanc. Pierre then sent one Frenchman into the village to see if any Germans were there. The Frenchman returned and reported, "There are no Germans in the village. There are only the villagers, and all in town is quiet." Two men remained behind guarding the dynamite, fuses, and other material, while the other 22 went into a coffee shop in the village.

About 20 minutes later, while the men in the coffee shop were drinking wine and coffee, they heard lots of commotion outside. It was the sound of approaching trucks, cars, and three pieces of artillery. The Germans were stopping about 50 meters from the coffee shop. They numbered 106 men.

The Frenchmen were taken by surprise. They didn't even have their weapons; they had left them behind. Pierre gave orders for no one to move. He instructed everyone to stay put and eat and drink at his table in a natural manner. Meanwhile, the Germans left their artillery outside with 5 guards and headed for the coffee shop. Upon entering the restaurant, the Germans assumed the Frenchmen were part of the French police. As the Frenchmen were wearing their civilian clothes, the Germans had no reason to fear they were resistance fighters. In fact, the Germans asked them if there were any terrorists in the village. The reply was "No."

While the Germans relaxed, Pierre calmly gestured for everyone to go outside the restaurant, one or two at a time. After about ten minutes, all the Frenchmen were outside. They immediately went for their weapons. Quickly, Pierre came up with a plan. He told his men, "Before the Germans move, we'll encircle the whole village." They encircled the village, setting up machine guns at four different points. The group aimed their weapons at the German trucks, the five German guards, and the restaurant. The moment one German moved, they would be able to kill him instantly. Alex operated one of the four machine guns. One Frenchman was sent to warn the villagers to stay off the streets.

When some of the Germans began to walk out of the restaurant, the Frenchmen threw grenades onto one of the trucks. The truck immediately burst into flames and exploded. More Germans quickly came running from the coffee shop and went for the other trucks and artillery. However, they weren't fast enough. The Frenchmen killed them. One of the Germans handling the artillery became so excited that he fired an artillery shell into one of the homes. He didn't have time to set the artillery in the proper direction. He, too, was killed as well as the other guards left with the remaining artillery and trucks. After a few minutes, the remaining Germans in the coffee shop came outside and surrendered.

Rules

The Frenchmen killed a total of 17 Germans. They took the other 89 as prisoners. One German escaped, but after a day or two, another group captured him. At first, the Frenchmen wanted to kill all the prisoners, but the officers gave orders that the moment they surrendered they were not to kill them. Instead, the Frenchmen took the prisoners to another resistance group.

Alex recalled, "When we left this town near Blanc, we had so many German prisoners we didn't have the time or the men to take the artillery pieces." Although Alex's group was outnumbered at least 4 to 1, they had worked perfectly together to overcome the Germans.

Two weeks later, another resistance group brought five German prisoners to Alex's camp. Pierre asked Alex to be the prisoners' interpreter since Alex was the only one who could speak German. Alex questioned the Germans and interpreted the answers for Pierre. One of the prisoners had a big bandage on his left hand. Alex asked him, "What do you have under the bandaged hand?" He replied, "A wound." Alex replied, "Take the bandage off." But the prisoner refused. Again Alex told him, "Take the bandage off." Still he refused. So, Alex told two Frenchmen that he had to see what was under the bandage. They took the German and forced the bandage off his hand. Under the bandage they found many rings, gold, jewelry, and diamonds that had been stolen.

Alex remembered another mission in May 1944, during which he spotted three German soldiers. His group had just passed an open plain and was about to enter a forest. The Germans came toward them with their hands up. Pierre ordered, "Everyone stay down." He was all too cognizant of a similar event when some of his men had been killed. At that time, the Germans had managed to kill three Frenchmen while about nine others had escaped. Pierre was wise to the Germans' tricks.

Through Alex, Pierre told the Germans, "Come forward." The Germans, however, refused to come. Pierre ordered, "Open fire." The three Germans no sooner fell to the ground than the entire plain became filled with gunfire. The Germans had used the three men as decoys. Other Germans came out from the forest and opened fire. The French responded by returning fire. Meanwhile, Pierre ordered his men to divide into groups and encircle the Germans. One group was to come up on them from behind. Through this plan, the French killed several Germans and took 15 others as prisoners. Some Germans escaped.

Later that month, on a beautiful Sunday, Alex remembered being free with nothing to do. He left the camp and asked permission to go to Azay le Ferron. A Frenchman by the name of Lefevre accompanied him. They wore civilian clothes to avoid suspicion, traveling by the countryside roads. When they were about halfway to their destination, five French policemen, who were from Petain's police unit and collaborating with the Nazis, suddenly accosted Alex and Lefevre. They surprised them. Lefevre cautioned Alex, "Don't be frightened and don't move. Let me do the talking." The French policemen asked, "Who are you?" Lefevre replied, "We're from here, don't you recognize us?" At that same moment he put his hand in his pocket for proof and withdrew his revolver and directed it point blank at the policeman who was interrogating him. "I'll tell you who I am," Lefevre said. "Go back. Go on your way before I kill you. You're a Frenchmen and I'm a Frenchman. You have no business asking me who I am." At this point, the five French policemen were very frightened. Lefevre then warned them, "Go and don't ask any Frenchmen any more questions. The first one that looks back, I'll kill." They started on their way, and none of them turned back to look.

Alex and Lefevre spent a relaxing day in Azay le Ferron. Lefevre visited his parents, and Alex visited Mrs. Sally and her 18-year-old daughter Eva, who was a remarkably beautiful girl. Alex liked Mr. and Mrs. Sally very much, but he liked Eva the most. She also liked Alex. They went together whenever Alex came to town. However, he felt apprehensive about their friendship, partially because she was young but especially because she worked in an office with Germans who exploited her. Alex knew that she had slept with Germans and French on many occasions, but he never told her family.

That same day, Alex spent the afternoon visiting the Erdmans. They exchanged news and ate a big meal together. In the evening, Mr. Sally came back from work. His position in the village was taking care of the roads. The war was taking its toll on Mr. Sally, and everyone could see he was unhealthy and steadily growing worse. In the First World War, he had been wounded by shrapnel. This was still in his shoulder and caused him much pain. He couldn't work very hard, but he was a good man.

After that day, Alex didn't have time for more visits. His underground activities increased. On several occasions his group went for more supplies and ammunition, parachuted in by allied planes from England. Every evening they would set up wherever the enemy was known to pass.

Also during the spring of 1944, Alex remembered how he and the others traveled on horses at least 35 kilometers from the forest camp to a farm. When they reached the farm, they separated into two groups, each having 25 men. For several hours, they traveled up and down the mountains. They had a breathtaking view for many kilometers in each direction.

The officer in Alex's group told everyone to dismount for a rest. The men began cleaning their guns, as they didn't have much else to do. While a young French boy was cleaning the machine gun, he accidentally set off the charger. Alex ran over and pushed the boy's hand and finger away from the trigger; the terrified boy was unable to do it himself. When Alex inspected the machine gun chamber, he saw that none of the 24 bullets were left inside. Fortunately, no one was hurt in this incident.

One day that spring, two Frenchmen from Alex's group at Azay-le-Feron were transporting supplies. Using a bus, they took a side road where they didn't expect to encounter Germans. However, a German company surprised them. The two Frenchmen became panic-stricken. They made an attempt to escape with their bus, but the German soldiers immediately chased them down with motorcycles. When the Germans drew nearer and were about to overtake them, the Frenchmen stopped the bus and tried to escape into the forest. The Germans cut both of the men down dead.

The Germans began sending many new divisions to the southern part of France, expecting that the Allies would soon attack from southern France or Italy. Alex and the other resistance members observed the buildup of German divisions passing on the main roads in Indre.

Meanwhile, the Americans were bombing trains, making it hard for the Germans to move efficiently. Alex's group was certain that something would happen soon in southern France. Circulating rumors claimed that it would not be long before the Allies would land in Europe.

Before the Allies landed, two Frenchmen from the resistance were given a mission to travel from Blanc to Azay le Ferron. They took an old car. Anyone not working with the Germans was to put a white star on the top of their car. This signal would protect cars from being bombed by the Americans. Since the two Frenchmen's car didn't have a star, the Americans thought they were Germans and bombed the car. The French people tried to save them, but it was too late. Both men were dead.

Alex's underground group had orders from the Allies in Britain to paralyze German movements as much as possible. To that end, the group attempted to block roads and destroy bridges. They also endeavored to sabotage a train, but found it difficult because of the French police's rigid control of transport. However, other underground groups also had men working to sabotage the trains. Due to their knowledge of where the German and French guards were positioned, other groups were more successful in detonating trains.

By early June 1944, the Germans started to attack French partisans, using spies in their efforts. One of Alex's friends caught a suspicious Frenchman named Charboneau. Alex's friend was convinced that he was a spy working for the Germans. At first Charboneau wouldn't talk. The French, then, beat him so badly that his face became spattered with blood. Since he still wouldn't talk, they put him in a pig shelter where he sat for a whole week. Each day he was beaten, but he remained adamant and silent. One day they beat Charboneau so brutally that Alex wanted to intervene. Alex was afraid that they would kill him.

Alex felt pity for Charboneau, even though he might have been a German spy. This was still no reason to beat him so badly, he reflected. Alex considered killing Charboneau to end his suffering, but he was afraid his friends might think that he too was working with the Germans. The underground would torture and kill every collaborator. But the Germans would respond by torturing and killing partisans. Alex therefore told himself, "It's better that this be none of my business."

It was still early June one evening when two young brothers, who were students from an aristocratic family, were placed to guard Charboneau, who was sitting in the pig house. Alex, meanwhile, finished his guard duty in another place at 10 p.m. He walked to the place where the two young brothers stood guard.

After observing the boys' lack of caution, he told them, "If you're not careful, you'll fall asleep."

Alex secretly went about 9 meters further, turned around, looked, and saw Charboneau constantly watching the two to see whether they would fall asleep. Less than a half-hour passed and both boys were sound asleep. Alex approached Charboneau and warned, "You move and I'll kill you." He took the two guns and hid them from the students. Then he watched Charboneau so he wouldn't escape. The two students slept for about two hours and didn't know anything even happened. Charboneau would certainly have killed both boys if it hadn't been for Alex.

When the brothers awoke, Alex decided to give them a lesson regarding the seriousness of their responsibilities and the potential consequences of not doing a good job. He told them, "Do you know Charboneau escaped? Your very life was in danger. Where are your guns?" Not knowing that Charboneau hadn't escaped, they realized their mistake. They promised they would amend their ways and Alex said he wouldn't report it to Commandant Carol. Alex gave them a second chance. He later commented, "These boys were very educated, but not for the underground."

On the 6th of June 1944, the partisans had big and joyful news: the Allies had landed in France. [1] Again, Alex's group had orders to harass the Germans and not let them pass from the north to the south. Alex's group didn't concentrate on trains, for the American bombers struck unceasingly at all the trains in France. Consequently, all locomotive movement was curtailed.

Carol informed his men, "From now on, we'll sleep very little. We'll sleep only during the day. At night we have ambushes to carry out." The small resistance group of approximately 130 men never stayed in the same place. They operated as far as 100 kilometers away from their campsite, hampering the Germans' movement. Each night, Alex's group blew up bridges or blocked roads with trees.

After the Allies landed, the Germans began surrendering in large numbers. In mid-June, one of the Frenchmen brought a prisoner named Fritz into camp. Fritz was between the ages of 40 and 45. He couldn't speak one word of French and, consequently, Alex was brought in as an interpreter. Fritz was scared because he believed that the underground fighters were going to kill him. Alex asked Fritz, "Where do you come from?" He replied, "Bremen." Alex told him he knew Bremen well. Among many questions, he asked, "From what battalion are you? Where is your division?" During his questioning of Fritz, Alex assured him, "If you answer, we won't kill you." Fritz was more than glad to respond to all his questions.

Since the partisans wouldn't give food to anyone unless they worked, Alex told Fritz, "You'll work in the kitchen." Alex had other concerns than Fritz's need for food. He knew that if Fritz had nothing to do, he'd try to escape. So Alex kept him busy and Fritz was glad to work. In fact, he said, "Give me more work. I'll do a good job." As a result, Alex couldn't remember having such well-shined shoes. In exchange for Fritz's work, Alex followed through on his promise to feed him. However, Alex cautioned, "If you try to escape, we'll kill you." After one day at the camp, Fritz was taken away with the other prisoners. Before he departed, he thanked Alex for saving his life.

XXII

the Forest de Prailly

During July 1944, the Germans killed two Frenchman from Azay le Feron in a nearby forest area. Alex's group planned their burial for the following Sunday. One Frenchman, Lefrand, who knew Alex was free that Sunday, came to him and asked, "Alex, will you take my guard today? I'd like to go to the funeral of my friends who were killed." Alex replied, "All right, I'll take your place. Where do you have to be stationed?" Lefrand told him, "In the Forest de Prailly." Alex then wanted to know what time he would return. Lefrand answered, "I'll be gone from 9 a.m. to 6 p.m." On the burial day, Alex and his group of six young Frenchmen between the ages of 18 and 22 traveled about ten kilometers of dirt road from the camp and came to the main asphalt road in the Forest de Prailly. Alex set his machine gun facing the corner where the two roads intersected. Although their position was in dense forest, an open plain was directly visible on the other side of the dirt road.

From 8 a.m. until noon, they waited and nothing happened; all was quiet. It was a beautiful day. Every two hours, Alex changed the man who was positioned on the other side of the road. At noon they ate well. Alex then told them, "You can all take a short rest, but be ready just in case." Alex sent Martin Filipp to stand guard on the other side of the road where the open plain was. Alex cautioned him, "If you see anything, come over and tell me right away. Above all, be sure no one sees you."

Alex had 17 rounds of ammunition. Each round comprised about 25 bullets. While the five young Frenchmen rested, Alex loaded one round into the machine gun. Finally, Alex, too, decided to take a half-hour rest from 12:30 to 1:00 p.m.

Suddenly, sometime shortly after 1:00 p.m., Alex heard a loud noise. Forty "panzer wagons" came down the road preceded by a small private officer's car. The car stopped precisely at the point where the dirt road intersected with the asphalt road, directly in front of Alex's emplacement. After all the panzer wagons stopped, the officer got out of the front car and shouted, "Afsteigen," meaning "Everyone get out of the trucks."

Immediately, all the soldiers sprang from the wagons. They headed for the open field, which was directly in front of Alex but across the dirt road. Alex noticed that the soldiers were all SS troops. They were thin and very young, aged 19 to 22. Alex was taken by surprise. It had all happened so quickly that he had no time to think. When the soldiers were 14 or 18 meters across the open field, Alex turned his machine gun and aimed his five bullets at the officer and private car. However, he had no time to observe the results. He then started to shoot into the open field, feeding the ammunition into the machine gun with his left hand. Wherever he saw two or more men running he would fire. He finished one charger, then a second charger, a third charger, and so on. In a matter of minutes, he had finished all 17 rounds of ammunition.

With so many of their men falling, the Germans returned to their trucks and began firing artillery shells towards the forest. To Alex's advantage, the Germans didn't know exactly where his gunfire was coming from, because he was completely protected by trees. As a result, the bullets repeatedly missed him. Instead, they hit some of the trees surrounding him; pieces of one tree even fell on him.

When Alex found that he was down to his last two or three bullets, he realized that there was nothing more he could do there. With grenades falling within 9 or 14 meters of him, he knew he needed to move. He remembered his orders, "Don't make direct war. Hit and run." He grabbed his machine gun with the remaining bullets and started to head back into the dense forest. He didn't lift his head up, but ran in a crouched position. After moving back 27 or more meters, he knew the Germans wouldn't see or find him. He felt safer. He knew the bullets couldn't reach him because of the forest.

Alex returned to an established rendezvous point he had made with the six young Frenchmen, but he didn't find anyone there. Later, he found out that the Frenchmen hadn't shot even one bullet. When Martin Filipp, the one on guard, saw the Germans, he began to flee across the dirt road until a bullet wounded his left ankle. The five other Frenchmen assisted him and together they retreated to safety.

Alone, Alex then decided to return to his underground camp six kilometers away. He had to pass two tiny dirt roads. When he reached the first dirt road, he observed German soldiers racing toward him. They were only 180 meters away so he had to act quickly. He hurriedly sprang from one side of the road to the other.

The Germans fired at him, barely missing his body by a few centimeters. Alex fled into the forest. After running some 300 meters, he glanced back. He realized that he was again safe; the forest was so overgrown that they couldn't find him.

In this dense forest, Alex heard constant gunfire coming from his camp. He estimated that there were 100 or more people exchanging gunfire. He realized that the Germans must have attacked his friends.

While in the impenetrable forest, Alex was suddenly frightened by a loud noise directly behind him. His heart stopped for a second. He turned around to look, and there he saw a beautiful deer about two meters tall with huge antlers. When the deer saw Alex, he sprang into the air right over Alex's head. Alex recalled, "I never before saw such a big and beautiful deer." Once he realized that the noise came from a deer, he felt better.

Alex became concerned that the Germans might burn the forest area where he was hiding. He continued to walk within one kilometer of his camp, passing the second dirt road. At this point, he observed a group of Germans about 270 meters away. He again lunged across the road, but this time crossed before they could see him.

When Alex was about 90 meters from his camp, he confirmed his suspicion that his camp was under attack. The exchange of gunfire was still very strong, and he heard deafening noise. He couldn't figure out how he could safely get into the camp. Realizing that some Germans were known to climb trees to kill people passing beneath, he constantly looked up, but there was no movement in the trees.

About 9 to 14 meters from the camp he stopped for a few minutes. He was both alarmed and frightened. It was now about 3:30 p.m. He wanted to get to the ammunition in his camp. He knew there was plenty, if only he could get to it. Lying hidden in the thick bushes, he saw and heard several Germans in an open space leaning over another German. One German said, "Hey Franz, get up." Another German responded, "Aw, this guy is finished." After about 10 minutes, Alex could still hear the sound of ammunition being fired. He knew that it would be impossible to get back to the camp and decided to retreat back into the forest for safety.

Once in the forest, he searched for a way out. He didn't know his exact location but was certain he was heading in the right direction. It was about 7 p.m.; the sun was quickly dropping in the sky. At last, at about 7:45 p.m., he saw a small farmhouse about 180 meters from the forest. He didn't know whether he should go to the farmhouse or not. He told himself, "I'll put my gun somewhere. I won't take the gun inside while asking for directions." He looked for the largest tree and then looked at the house. He hid the gun under the tree and covered it with grass.

Then, as he was about to leave the forest, his inner voice told him, "Alex, don't! Don't go! If you go to that house, there's great danger!" He said to himself, "I will go!" Again he heard, "If you go, you'll be in trouble!" Three or four meters from the end of the forest, he again started towards the farmhouse. He later recalled, "Something took me back." Again the internal warning said, "Don't go!" Alex decided, after much deliberation, that it was better not to go.

He looked in another direction and saw a little village. Under the cover of the encroaching forest, he approached a narrow dirt road that led into the village. He found the alley to be clear and started walking toward the village. After going about 50 meters, he suddenly heard bullets flying over his head and immediately hit the ground. Looking around, he saw nothing but the village. He didn't know where the bullets had come from. No one came out of the forest.

After waiting 10 minutes and not seeing anyone move toward him, he stood up. He resumed his hike towards the village, which he was later to find out was Prailly. After he walked another 50 meters, bullets grazed his head. He again dropped to the ground. He looked around to see if he could find anyone, but no one appeared. He supposed the shots must have come from his side. To one side, he could see the very same farmhouse he had almost entered. The Germans were hiding there. This explained the sporadic gunfire in his direction. Anyone entering that farmhouse would have walked into a trap and surely would have been killed.

Alex began to run, stopping at the first farm he came across. He asked the farmer, "Are there any Germans here?" The farmer answered, "Leave at once. I beg you to leave at once. I don't want you endangering my family for one second." Alex saw a water pump. He dashed for the pump, drank some water, and ran from the farm. He headed down an asphalt road until he reached a park in the village of Les Mesles. He climbed a six-foot fence and fell near some beautiful flowers on the other side. Walking in the park for several meters, he saw many children between 10 and 15 years old watching their cows. At first they were alarmed, but Alex told them, "Don't be frightened." Alex then asked them, "What village am I in?" They replied, "You are in Les Mesles." He then asked them, "How can I get to Azay le Ferron?" They told him he was about nine kilometers from Azay le Ferron and explained how he could get there.

Alex followed their directions. About one kilometer down a lonely road, he saw a woman about 60 or 70 years old watching her three pigs in an adjacent field. She saw him approach her. When he came near, Alex said, "Bon Soir." She thought he was an Englishman because he was wearing the English uniform commonly worn by the French underground. She asked him, "Did you come from the forest?" He replied, "Yes. How can I get to Azay le Ferron?" She answered, "Not here, not here. We must not talk here; we must go in the house. She led Alex into the house and advised him not to go outside. The woman noticed that Alex was scratched and bloody. He was perspiring heavily, hot, and thirsty. When he asked her for something to drink, she brought him food and wine.

She asked him, "Can you tell me what happened in the forest?" Alex replied, "I don't know." The entire time that Alex was in this lady's home, he could hear sporadic gunfire and loud noises in the distance. He was anxious because there was a massive amount of

Alex in Underground attire with Commandant Carol.

ammunition in his resistance camp. The woman then told Alex, "Look, you have to change out of the English army uniform you have on. Put on these civilian clothes. First you change; you can't leave in army clothes." He replied, "All right." She also said, "You don't have to be frightened here. You were lucky. The Germans aren't going to move quickly. If you go to the camp, they'll capture you and probably kill you."

Bothered by something, and knowing that Alex came from the forest, she asked, "Did you know Lefrand?" "Sure," Alex replied. "Lefrand was the man whose place I took this morning. I know him. You don't have to worry." She asked Alex, "Are you sure he wasn't in the forest? How did this happen?" Alex answered, "He went to the funeral. I' m 100 percent certain he wasn't in the forest when the Germans laid siege to the camp." The woman was elated. Later, she told Alex that she was Lefrand's aunt. "You can't move from here now," she said. Alex insisted, "But I have to go to Azay le Ferron."

She asserted, "You can go when it's dark at night around 10 or 11 p.m. An old man will come along who knows the forest well. He'll direct you to a path where it will be easy for you."

In the late dark of evening, the old man came and accompanied Alex to a farmhouse. It was still night when they reached the farmhouse. Near the forest, the old man spoke. "I'll ask if it's possible for you to sleep here," he said. Alex replied, "It's not necessary. From here I know the road. I don't want to sleep here." The old man advised Alex, "If you follow this path you'll find the road to Azay le Ferron."

The stars became brighter as the morning drew a new sky. In a short time it would be daybreak. The old man received permission to sleep in the farmhouse, and Alex continued on the path toward Azay le Ferron. Alex arrived at Mr. Pournin's farm in Les Mesles when it was still dark. He didn't go inside the house, deciding it was best to sleep outside the farm near the stable.

As the sun began to rise, Alex realized he couldn't sleep anymore. While awaking, he saw Madeline coming towards him with pails to milk the cows. He met her and said, "Bonjour, Madeline." She turned towards him, half-frightened and not knowing him. "Madeline," Alex declared. "Don't you recognize me?" "No," she replied. "Who are you?" Alex answered, "I'm John." (John was Alex's name on the Pournin's farm.)

She responded, "John! John's been killed!" She believed Alex was dead. "But look at me," Alex replied. "I'm alive, not dead." She came closer and saw Alex was black from ammunition and scratched and bloody from escaping the forest. After gazing at him for a minute, she spoke. "You mean the Germans didn't kill you?" The girl dropped her two pails and ran hurriedly into the farmhouse, shouting, "Mr. Pournin, Mr. Pournin, John is here!"

In a matter of seconds, the Pournins got up out of bed, stormed from the house, ran down the steps, and exclaimed, "Are you really John? What happened?" "It's great luck seeing you, John," Mrs. Pournin said as she led him inside the house. Alex then told them all that had transpired. Mr. Pournin informed Alex that all the officers, including Lt. Pierre, had come and told them that he had been killed. All the people in Azay le Ferron also believed he was dead.

In Prailly, Alex found out that no one at the camp had been killed. The orders in the camp had been to escape. Everyone had indeed escaped; however, many Germans had been killed in their siege of the camp. The Germans couldn't understand how not one Frenchman had been killed. However, the French underground camp had lost an enormous amount of ammunition.

On a morning in late July at the Pournin's home, Alex heard from Radio London that 36 Germans had been killed in the Forest de Prailly in Indre. Alex didn't go to Azay le Ferron right away, but stayed at the Pournin's farm where he slept until noon. During lunch, Mr. Pournin told Alex, "Pierre is in a house only one kilometer from here. He sent someone over to tell Pierre that Alex had returned. After he received the news, Pierre arrived within 30 minutes. He embraced Alex and asked many questions. Alex told him exactly what had happened. Pierre said, "We found the road where you demolished the officer's private car. It was completely broken. We also have evidence that many Germans were killed, for there was a lot of blood." Pierre then advised him, "Tomorrow, we'll regroup. I'll come and pick you up." Alex asked Pierre, "Are there any Germans in Azay le Ferron?" Pierre replied, "No, when do you want to go?" "Today," replied Alex. Pierre agreed, "You can go."

That same afternoon, Alex went to Azay le Ferron to visit his cousins Mr. and Mrs. Sally and the Erdman's. When Mrs. Erdman saw Alex, she cried for several minutes before she could speak

Alex marching in French Resistance uniform with the 17ᵗʰ light infantry unit and Commandant Carol.

clearly. She thought she was seeing someone who was dead. Alex's friends and family had a big celebration and ate dinner together. As Alex put it, "When Frenchmen like somebody they really show it." Alex ate well and drank excellent wine. He stayed late into the evening.

Alex returned to the Pournin's farm that night. The next day, Pierre came and picked up Alex. They traveled to a new camp in the forest. Alex never asked many questions from then on. At the camp, no one could understand how Alex could have killed so many Germans or how he survived. He had faced an entire army, about 100 men, alone. Although he was only 18 meters away, the Germans were unable to kill him.

For the first three days after his attack, Alex's group had orders to hide out. They were instructed not to move their position because the Germans were actively doing surveillance work. Those three days were terribly trying for the men; they had nothing to eat but bread and water and almost starved to death. During this time, Commandant Carol explained to Alex how the Germans burned all their ammunition during a surprise attack. As Alex suspected, it was this attack that he had heard while seeking shelter from Lefrand's aunt. Carol said, "We couldn't take much with us. Fortunately no one was hurt." Then he asked, "Where is your machine gun?" Alex told him, "I had to leave it near a farmhouse close to the forest in Prailly."

Carol asked one officer to go with Alex to look for the machine gun. Dressed in civilian clothes, the two men walked for several hours until they reached the farmhouse. Alex then looked for the biggest tree and measured the distance from this tree to the house to be sure it was the right house. He returned to the tree and began furiously scratching and clawing the grass and dirt with his hands. The officer thought Alex was crazy, until he saw the machine gun protruding from the ground. They placed the gun in a dark potato bag and took it to their new camp in the forest. Appreciating Alex's efforts, some of the men commented, "You must be a real soldier, Alex. No one would ever carry an empty gun so far."

By the summer of 1944, the French took many German prisoners who were very willing to surrender. Sometimes one, two, or three Germans came into one of the nearby villages and requested to be taken prisoner. At other times, a group of Germans would come looking for something to steal, and in the process would be killed. By this stage in the war, many French people were volunteering to join the resistance.

XXIII

return to Paris

In mid-August 1944, the Allies entered Paris, and the Germans surrendered the city.[1] Alex received permission from Commandant Carol to go to Paris. The trip took Alex three and a half days. He had to hitchhike because all the trains were at a standstill. In addition to the train problems, the movements of American troops further slowed his journey over a bridge. For four hours, Alex stood by and watched the United States Army columns advance with tanks and artillery. Alex didn't mind the delay. Instead, he felt very thrilled to see the Americans. He commented, "I had never seen so many weapons and ammunition before."

While traveling to Paris, Alex also saw hundreds of free horses roaming through the fields near Orleans. About 100 kilometers from Paris, he saw a U.S. Army camp. It was evening and the American soldiers were eating supper. The army stayed at camp that night and began to march out the following morning. Alex was surprised to see the Americans consuming so much gasoline, because it was so scarce and expensive in France during the war. French civilians weren't allowed to own or drive a car. [2]

When Alex arrived in Paris, he saw many old Frenchmen who were delighted that the Allies had arrived. However, life was very difficult there. There was a lot of sadness. Many people had been deported or imprisoned. Many were hungry or cold. [3] Although the war had ended, France still suffered from severe shortages of food and coal.[4] It was difficult to obtain a meal. In order to get food, you needed an alimentation card issued by the city of Paris.

The sights of Paris had also been affected by the war. Wherever Alex went, he saw that the bronze from all the monuments was missing. The stone was still there, but the beautiful bronze had been taken by the Germans to make bullets. Similarly, military debris scattered the banks of the Seine. [5] There was a feeling of emptiness.

Soon after Alex's return, Mr. and Mrs. Erdman arrived in Paris. They discovered that their apartment at 18 Rue de l'Etoile was occupied. The Erdman's told the new occupants, "This is our apartment, and we'll have this apartment back." They lived in a hotel for a month while the court decided the case. The judge ruled in the Erdman's' favor and ordered the other residents to vacate the premises. Alex started to work with Erdman. They were unable to work in the grocery business as they had before because there were no eggs, butter, meat, or any other groceries to sell. The two men returned into the black market. Alex lived dangerously again.

In the old Jewish sector, many Jews slowly began organizing the clothing factories. Others became active in the black market by buying and selling cigarettes, candy, and so forth. On one occasion, Erdman told Alex, "Go to Strasbourg. You'll only have to be there one day. Take this suitcase containing German marks. You'll meet an American sergeant there." He instructed him to go to a particular monument and said, "When the sergeant comes to you and says his name, give him the suitcase. He'll give you one packet of French francs in return."

Alex did as he was advised. It took him three days to accomplish this mission in Strasbourg. He made enough money from this one trip to live for at least a month. Another time, Erdman sent Alex to receive a packet with 36 French francs. Alex waited at the pre-arranged meeting point. After waiting and watching for 20 minutes, one man met him and gave him two packets instead of one. Alex brought the two packets back to Erdman. One franc was missing.

After examining the packets and finding only 35 pieces, Erdman asked Alex, "Did you lose one piece?" Alex replied, "No." After checking with the man with whom he had dealt, Erdman found out that he had in fact only given Alex 35 pieces. After this incident all the Jewish people trusted Alex and he received many jobs. He usually took his bicycle or the subway to accomplish these tasks.

Alex marching with his French Resistance Unit.

After a while, Alex thought about what could happen if the police caught him. He realized, "I'll sit in prison all my life. I don't need this or want this to happen." He then went to Erdman and said, "I'm going to find another job." Just about that time, the Americans in Paris were asking for people to do office work. Alex went to the Champs d' Elysee. An American female officer was interviewing applicants. She said to Alex, "We need people." Alex informed her, "But I don't even speak English." She replied, "It's not necessary that you know English. It's enough that you know French and German."

Three days later, he reported to his new job and was given the task of preparing documents for German war prisoners. Alex separated the names of the prisoners by their rank, address, age, division, and company. He did this for six months, between December 1944 and June 1945. Alex always ate in the same lunchroom with the American soldiers. He recalled, "At that time, it was difficult to eat that well even in the best restaurants in France."

Alex was a quick and industrious worker. His supervisor, an American sergeant named Blackie, watched Alex go about his duties. Alex rarely saw the Commander in the office, only once every two or three weeks. Blackie treated Alex well, giving him American candy, and once giving him a new American pen. Alex went out into the street and sold the pen for three times what it was worth.

Because Blackie treated Alex so well, Alex hurriedly retrieved whatever documents Blackie needed. For assistance, Alex said that he relied upon the many French women who "liked to do that kind of work." He just needed to explain what kind of document was needed. With their help, he could quickly bring documents to Blackie. Blackie was always pleased that Alex completed his work so efficiently.

By the time his job was finished, Alex had seen many documents from Hitler and all the main German generals and officers, down to the least known privates. All these papers passed through his hands. Sometimes Blackie took Alex to a restaurant in a Jeep. It was then that Blackie would tell him, "Alex, you have to go to America to live someday." Alex replied, "Maybe I will if it's ever possible, but after the war is over I plan on returning to Poland."

When the war ended and Poland was presumably free, Alex wrote to the Swiss Red Cross requesting any news or information about his parents and sisters in Poland. A letter soon came to him from a Jewish organization. The letter stated, "Nobody from your family lives in Stary Soncz, Poland. The very moment we find their whereabouts, we will write to you." Alex never received another letter from this organization.

After the liberation of France, Andre, whom Alex and all the other men loved so very much because of her beauty, also came to Paris. The French partisans in Azay le Ferron had taken six girls who had slept with the Germans and cut off all their hair, including Andre's. This was common treatment for women who were believed to have been too friendly with the Germans.[6]

Although Alex liked Andre, he realized she lacked intelligence and he wasn't interested in pursuing a relationship with her. Andre was only 18 years of age. She had one French boyfriend in Azay le Ferron, but he had broken up with her before the Germans had come to Azay le Ferron. It was then that she started sleeping with all kinds of men, including Germans.

In Paris, Andre told Alex, "After six months, I'll have my hair back. I didn't lose anything." She went about wearing a blonde wig until her hair grew back. Andre lived for a while with Mrs. Erdman and worked in the Erdmans' new coffee shop, Erdman and Rozof Coffee Shop. Rozof was a very wealthy Russian Jew with whom Erdman had formed a business partnership.

*A Red Cross letter sent to Alex in March of 1945 informing him
that his family was nowhere to be found in Poland.*

When the war ended on the European front in May 1945, Alex
left his office job; he didn't care for that kind of work. He began
working as an electrician and soon had more than enough work to
do. His work was mostly in Jewish apartments for Jewish clientele.

When Alex inspected the apartments, he found all the electric copper wires missing. Consequently, his clients didn't have
any electricity, and Alex had more work than he could handle.
Although copper wire was difficult to obtain, Alex knew of one
source. However, copper wire was sold at a higher price than aluminum wire. As long as his customers were willing to pay the
price, he could obtain the wire. Many Jews trusted Alex and called
on him for all of their electrical installation work.

XXIV

exodus to Israel

In October 1945, Alex received a letter from his brother Emanuel, who was living in Israel. Emmanuel asked Alex to come to Israel, but Alex had no desire to go there at that time. Instead, Alex told him that everything was all right in Paris and he liked it there. He asked Emmanuel to move to Paris.

Emanuel replied to Alex's letter, telling him that he was married and had two children, and therefore it was too difficult for him to move. He also wrote, "I'm in a kibbutz. It's a quiet life. I like my work, driving a truck, which is not difficult. I like it here. I don't wish to move."

Alex decided to stay in Paris for the time being. He had plenty of work as an electrician. He hired two workers, one Jewish and one French Catholic, to assist him with his increasing workload. Alex paid them very well. While in Paris, Alex dated his cousin Jacqueline Schenkman. After a lengthy courtship, she told Alex, "I like you, but I don't want to marry you." Alex informed her, "If you don't wish to marry me someday, then we won't go together anymore. After today, it's all over. I don't wish to see you anymore." The next day she came to see Alex, but he told her, "Go away, it's all over."

Soon after breaking up with Jacqueline, Alex learned about a Jewish organization in Paris located on Rue Ville de Temple. At this organization, he was able to meet Jews from different countries. In particular, he met several Jews from Poland. The organization provided meals. Alex remembered that the food and soup were delicious. One of the members encouraged Alex. "You can come here," he said. "We're organizing Jewish people to go to Israel." Alex was very interested in going to Israel by this time, but he didn't want to go alone. He feared isolation and loneliness. It was in this organization that Alex met his future bride, Marie Rachel Goltz. Marie was from Paris. She had lost all of her family and friends in the concentration camps.

Marie remembered how she felt when she first met Alex. She thought he had a dynamic personality. "He seemed very courageous, always wanting to help others," she said. "He was very athletic and used a bike for transportation." Marie remembered being especially impressed with his appetite. "It was interesting seeing a person with such a voracious appetite always asking for more food, soup or meat, and knowing what to say to obtain more." She noted that, "Although Alex was a foreigner, he made it okay with the language."

Marie remembered how she became better acquainted with Alex. Alex used to take her to visit his relatives the Erdman's, who showed her pictures of Alex's family. After a while, Alex thought they should get married. At first, Marie said that she wasn't sure about the idea because she didn't have any family. However, after a period of indecisiveness, they married. Throughout their marriage, she found that he always seemed to be troubled and hurt but didn't tell her what had happened to his family, as thought it was something he couldn't understand himself. She said, "He never told me what happened in real life.

Regarding the organization that sponsored their meals, Marie was never sure whether it was part of the Red Cross or a Jewish group. "It was a busy and interesting place, a kind of melting pot of the times. There were lots of refugees from different countries waiting to emigrate someplace in the world," she said. "There were people who didn't have any more family, people who were waiting for some news from their family or someone they used to know, and people in transit waiting for some news from a deported family. We were all feeling the same sadness even if we were strangers."

Meanwhile, Emmanuel kept insisting that Alex come to Israel. Finally Alex told him, "All right. Since you insist, I'll come." By that time, Alex and Marie had their first baby, Emanuel, only a couple of months old. Marie was anxious to leave France. She recalled, "The winter of 1947 was such a cold one. I couldn't wait to go someplace warmer. The water was freezing in the pipes. I would go anyplace to get warm, even Africa. Not knowing what was awaiting us, we were thinking of getting away temporarily to visit."

Alex found that his Jewish organization in Paris made all the travel plans for him and other Jewish refugees. In fact, most of the refugees didn't have to pay the full fare. Wealthy immigrants from other countries such as Germany and Austria supported them with the necessary finances.[1]

Jews had been immigrating into Palestine since the British Mandate of 1918, when Britain established Palestine as a home for Jewish people from around the world.[2] Since Britain only permitted about one-third of the immigration requests, Jews migrated illegally as well. This illegal migration was known as the "Aliya Bet Movement." The first ship of illegal immigrants arrived in 1934. With the help of Zionist organizations and private entrepreneurs,

Jews migrated into Palestine in various ways: legally, as visitors, and illegally with forged visas and fictitious marriage contracts or by surreptitious entrance across the shores.[3]

When World War II began, Aliya Bet faced insurmountable problems, such as limited financial resources, the increasing prices of ships, and severe government restrictions. In 1941 and 1942, Aliya Bet was unable to function. However, after the war ended, Aliya Bet became well organized and was supported by the influence of Holocaust survivors. Volunteers operated the ships. Others helped the new immigrants onto shore and into settlements, minimizing chances of detection by British authorities. Of the 530,000 immigrants who fled to Palestine until it became the state of Israel, Aliya Bet brought 25 percent, or 130,000.[4]

There were immigration centers throughout Europe staffed by Aliya Bet members from Palestine, also known as "Mosad." At these centers, the Mosad organized the refugees and made the necessary financial and political arrangements for departure. France was the center of Mosad's operations. More specifically, France was the gathering point for children from the Netherlands and Belgium as well as for all Jews from displaced persons' camps. Due to the deep-seated traditional antagonism of French officials toward the British, the Mosad found a political advantage being located in France.[5] Events that may have contributed to this antagonism include the perceived British abandonment of the French in June 1940, and Britain's ultimatum to the French fleet the following month to join their fleet or be sunk by them. Upon refusing, the French lost 1,147 sailors off the coast of Mers-El-Kebir, a French naval base in northwestern Algeria.[6]

Alex and Marie were given both a French passport and a British visa to Israel. When they received their visas, they were forewarned to not say anything if the British stopped them but to respond with as few words as possible. After obtaining the visas, they spent another week traveling to Marseilles where they waited for their ship. Many people were traveling to different destinations. After about three weeks, their ship arrived. Alex, Marie, and their baby boarded a Greek vessel called the Marathon and reached Haifa, Israel in December 1947.

Alex was lucky because many ships were caught. When this happened, British authorities forced the ships to return to their European ports or to detention camps in Cyprus. Fifty-two thousand immigrants were deported to Cyprus and detained until 1948 when Israel became a state. [7]

After Alex had been in Israel a short time, he found out to be true what his soul had feared and suspected for a long time. Back in 1943, Hawrilo had told him that his parents were missing. Now he received a letter from an old high school friend, Thadeuz Sefchick of Stary Soncz. Thadeuz wrote that it was very difficult to live in Poland in post-war years. He said, "If you are willing, I'll sell the Rosenfeld home, field, and factory."

Alex wrote back, "I'm going to return to Poland once the communists leave." Sefchick then described in conscientious and vivid detail the disheartening tragedy of his entire family. His mother and three sisters were shot, together with the other Jews in the village, in the forest between Stary Soncz and Nowy Soncz. Thadeuz also told him that someone who knew his father saw him alive in a lime factory named Libanon, near Krakow. However, he said that the Nazis later hanged his father. Alex learned that the Nazis kept his family alive until they were no longer needed, as they did with other Jews. His mind then went back to the train station in Krakow in 1936, and he remembered his mother's tears and words, "You know Alex, I know that I'll never see you again."

EPILOGUE

U pon arriving in Israel, Alex began a new life for himself and his family. No longer did he have to worry about Germans and concentration camps. Indicative of this change was the warm greeting that he received as he left the ship. His brother Emanuel had been waiting for him. After a long-anticipated reunion, Emanuel drove Alex and his family to his kibbutz, Kibbutz Kzvat.

At the kibbutz, they met Emanuel's wife Sarah, their two small children, Rivka and Neelie, and the other kibbutzniks. Marie remembered feeling happy to be on the kibbutz. She found it to be a "very nice organized place." Thinking about the winter in Europe, she was "glad to be someplace stable and warm." Compared with France, Israel's weather was much warmer.

Alex and Marie planned to make the kibbutz a temporary home. Their final destination was to be back in France, Marie's homeland. Over time, Alex and Marie slowly adjusted to the kibbutz. Marie explained that they had to learn a new language and new customs. Furthermore, soon after arriving, Marie delivered her second baby, Lillian.[1]

At the kibbutz, Alex soon discovered many new challenges. Arabs frequently threatened the kibbutz's security with gunfire. Consequently, the kibbutz needed his assistance to safeguard its people and property. Using his skills as a resistance fighter, Alex did whatever he could to protect the women, children, livestock, and crops. As in Europe, he continued to live a life filled with danger. Because of these obligations, Alex extended his visit at the kibbutz until his family had stayed for about a year.

Alex had other specific responsibilities. With his brother, he drove a 30 to 40 ton truck, transporting kibbutz products to Haifa markets and exchanging them for livestock feed. This was a dangerous job as the delivery route took them through mountainous territory where they were targets for Arab gunfire. To better secure themselves and the property, Alex built steel sides for the truck. With these structural modifications, he transformed the truck into a vehicle resembling the German panzer wagons that he had confronted back in the Forest de Prailly.

Besides driving the truck, Alex worked in the kibbutz machine shop. He used his welding skills as he had done in Europe.

While living on the kibbutz, Alex realized that its lifestyle wasn't for him. He wanted to earn more money and he wanted more independence. He resented not being allowed his own personal radio. He was told that if he wanted to listen to the news, he should go to the canteen and listen with the other kibbutznicks.

After leaving the kibbutz, Alex and his family moved to Haifa, where he worked as a plumber repairing sewer pipes. Without having a choice, he also enlisted in the army. By that time, the British mandate had expired and Israel had become an independent state. The Arabs were angry. There never was a Palestinian state. Israel's defense forces needed the help of young, strong men like Alex. Although Alex never liked being a soldier, he felt it was his duty as a Jew to protect Israeli territory.

In the army, he was often responsible for obtaining and loading ammunition as well as hiding ammunition under livestock food and in trucks and boats. To obtain ammunition, he often stole from United Nations soldiers' trucks and trains. He also frequently served on guard duty. Additionally, he utilized his previously acquired skills of welding, repairing and construction to build such things as heavy-duty metal containers to protect ammunition.

One of the Army's defense maneuvers that Alex participated in resembled a Bible story. It was a creative scheme that involved using loud noise to scare away the Arabs. In accordance with this scheme, Alex helped obtain and place hundreds of empty barrels at the top of Mt. Carmel. Everyone helped, men, women, and even children helped. They filled the barrels with rocks. When signaled, the Israelis threw the barrels down the mountain. As a result, they created a thunderous noise resembling cannons. The plan worked. The Arabs fled.

After completing his commitment of full-time army service, Alex still had to report one day per month and one full month per year. During these assignments, he did emergency repair work on broken-down trucks and cars, as well as boilers and weapons. As a civilian, he also worked for the army. His employer had a military contract requiring him to work in the Negev. This job involved a variety of mechanical work including building huge metal reservoirs for oil and gasoline tanks, as well as a new electrical station.

Apart from the army contract, Alex worked in Israel's refineries, providing plumbing and mechanical services.

After living in Israel for eight years, Alex decided he wanted to move his family to a place where they could lead a better life. Back in Poland, Alex's father had moved his family to Stary Soncz. For this same reason, Alex had a big move in mind; he now wanted to move to America. However, due to the needs of the Israeli army, Alex had to postpone this plan. He didn't leave Israel for another eight years.

Finally, in April 1963, Alex and his family left for America. By this, time, Alex and Marie had seven children: Emanuel, Lillian, Nathan, Viviane, Aliza, Alfred, and Irene. When Alex and his family arrived in the U.S. at Ellis Island, he had just $80 in his pockets.

As before, his brother Emanuel greeted him and his family. Unlike Alex, Emanuel had been able to leave Israel earlier because of health problems resulting from his years in Europe. For about four years, Alex worked at his brother's gas station. Then he moved to Rochester, New York and began working as an electrician for the University of Rochester. Alex died in 1992. His wife Marie and six children survived him. Alfred was among the first. Alfred tragically died in a fire. As of 2004, Alex's descendents included five grandchildren and two great grandchildren.

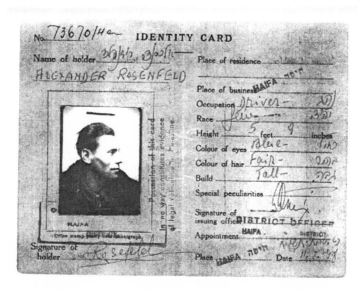

Card Alex received in Palestine that identified him as a driver.

מדינת ישראל

משרד הבטחון

אגף ליישוב החיילים ושקומם

הלשכה המקומית – חיפה

י"ח אייר תש"ט

17 למאי 1949

שק/1659.

לכבוד

מר רוזנפלד אלכסנדר,

רח' בית חולים מס' 28,

ח י פ ה .

א.נ.,

בקשתך מיום 22.2.49 לקבלת הלואה
בסך 300.– ל"י למטרת קניית כלים לביח
המלאכה שלך, נידונה בישיבה שהתקימה בח"א
באוצר החייל בע"מ ביום 2.5.49, ולאחר
בירור מקיף בבקשתך הגיעו לכלל מסקנה,
שאין ההלואה הכרחית לשקומך האישי ולכן
הוחלט לדחותה.

בכבוד רב,

אגף ליישוב החיילים ושקומם
הלשכה המקומית
ח י פ ה

חא/יפ

Unidentified document in Hebrew.

THE UNIVERSITY OF ROCHESTER

ROCHESTER, NEW YORK 14627
Dated October 10, 1944 at Azay le Ferron France

DEPARTMENT OF FOREIGN LANGUAGES,
LITERATURES AND LINGUISTICS

I, the undersigned, Rene Delacroix, local official of the Resistance and president of the Committee for Liberation, attest to having received on 20 November 1943, Mr. Alexander Rosenfeld, who, not wishing to return to Germany after expiration of his leave, was placed under my supervision with Mr. Louis Pournin at Mesles. During this period Mr. Rosenfeld showed a remarkable attitude; although only a few people knew him he was considered a friend, not a foreigner. His earnest wish to be of service was fulfilled when I had to help constitute a group of resistance fighters, the maquis underground. He entered the 17th light infantry under the command of Commandant Carol.

His willingness to serve and great bravery made him one of the best. Their camp, which had been set up in the Preuilly forest on June 6, 1944, was attacked by German guns and tanks on July 23 of that year. Mr. Rosenfeld, a group leader who was on guard, was the hero of the day. His men abandoned him after several minutes of combat but he continued to fire his machine gun causing great damage to the tanks fifty yards or so from his position.

When his ammunition was gone he had to withdraw under a hail of bullets and artillery fire, making sure to save his weapon. He was only able to rejoin his group by a very hazardous route under heavy enemy fire.

Mr. Rosenfeld had joined the Army in 1939 and when he left his underground group he asked to volunteer when it was to go up to the front line. His demobilization had been only temporary and it is natural that after the campaign in France, two years of forced labor in Germany and a period in the underground he should rest a bit.

I would like to add that Mr. Rosenfeld, an admirable young man in all respects, will be decorated for valor.

President of the Liberation Committee
of Azay- le- Ferron
Delacroix, postmaster

Certified by the mayor
Azay-le-Ferron
October 10, 1944
Signature and seal

Susan Man Jennings
SUSAN MAN JENNINGS
Notary Public in the State of New York
Monroe County   34761343
Commission Expires March 30, 19..?

Sworn to and signed before me on
this /7th day of March 1987.

I hereby declare that the above is a true and
and accurate translation to the best of my
knowledge.

Anne D. Lutkus

Anne D. Lutkus, Language Coordinator
Professor of French

Alex, wife Marie and their first two children, Lillian and Serge in Israel, 1949.

Azay le Ferron, le 10 Octobre 1944.

Je soussigné DELACROIX René, Responsable local de la Résistance et Président du Comité de Libération, certifie avoir reçu le 20 Novembre 1943, Monsieur ROSENFELD Alexandre, qui non désireux de rentrer en Allemagne à l'expiration de sa permission, a été placé par mes soins chez Mr POURNIN Louis à Mesles. Monsieur ROSENFELD a eu durant cette période une attitude remarquable puisque sa présence n'a été connu que d'un milieu très restreint où il est considéré non pas en étranger, mais en ami. Son ardent désir de servir a été comblé lorsque j'ai eu à aider à la constitution de maquis militaires. Il a été incorporé au 17ᵉ Chasseurs à pieds sous le commandement du Commandant Carol.

Son désir de bien faire et son extrême bravoure l'ont classé parmi les meilleurs. Le camp installé dans la forêt de Preuilly le 6 Juin 1944, a été attaqué par les Allemands le 23 Juillet 1944 au moyen de canons et d'autos blindées. Monsieur ROSENFELD chef de groupe et de garde ce jour, a été le héros de cette journée mémorable. Abandonné de ses hommes après quelques minutes de combat, il a continué seul à assurer le tir de son fusil mitrailleur, causant des ravages certains parmi les voitures stoppées à quelques vingtaines de mètres de son emplacement.

Ses munitions épuisées, il a dû replier sous une grêle de balles et d'obus, non sans emporter son arme et n'a pu rejoindre son groupe qu'après bien des péripéties et essuyé le feu de l'ennemi.

Monsieur ROSENFELD était engagé en 1939 et en quittant son groupe, a demandé à le rejoindre lorsqu'il montera en ligne. Sa démobilisation n'est que passagère et il est naturel qu'après sa campagne de France, 2 ans d'Allemagne comme travailleur et son passage au maquis, Monsieur ROSENFELD prenne quelque repos.

J'ajoute que, garçon parfait sous tous rapports, sera l'objet de citations méritées.

Le Responsable local
Président du Comité de Libération
d'Azay le Ferron

DELACROIX
Receveur des Postes.

Vu pour certification
Azay le Ferron le 10-10-1944
Le maire.
signature et cachet.

THE JEWISH LEDGER Thursday, December 3, 1987   Page 11

OPLE PEOPLE PEOPLE **PEOPLE** PEOPLE **PEOPLE**
OPLE PEOPLE PEOPLE **PEOPLE** PEOPLE **PEOPLE**

Alexander Rosenfeld, War Hero, Joins JWV

Dated October 10, 1944 at Azay le Ferron France

I, the undersigned, Rene Delacroix, local offical of the Resistance and president of the Committee for Liberation, attest to having received on 20 November 1943, Mr. Alexander Rosenfeld, who, not wishing to return to Germany after expiration of his leave, was placed under my supervision with Mr. Louis Pournin at Mesles. During this period Mr. Rosenfeld showed a remarkable attitude; although only a few people knew him he was considered a friend, not a foreigner. His earnest wish to be of service was fulfilled when I had to help constitute a group of resistance fighters, the maquis underground. He entered the 17th light infantry under the command of Commandant Carol.

His willingness to serve and great bravery made him one of the best. Their camp, which had been set up in the Preuilly forest on June 6, 1944, was attacked by German guns and tanks on July 23 of that year. Mr. Rosenfeld, a group leader who was on guard, was the hero of the day. His men abandoned him after several minutes of combat but he continued to fire his machine gun causing great damage to the tanks fifty yards of so from his position.

When his ammunition was gone he had to withdraw under a hail of bullets and artillery fire, making sure to save his weapon. He was only able to rejoin his group by a very hazardous route under heavy enemy fire.

Mr. Rosenfeld had joined the Army in 1939 and when he left his underground group he asked to volunteer when it was to go up to the front line. His demobilization had been only temporary and it is natural that after his campaign in France, two years of forced labor in Germany and a period in the underground he should rest a bit.

I would like to add that Mr. Rosenfeld, an admirable young man in all respects, will be decorated for valor.

President of the Liberation Committee of Azay-le-Ferron
Delacrois, postmaster
Certified by the mayor
Azay-le-Ferron
October 10, 1944
Signature and seal

Editor's Note: Alexander Rosenfeld, a resident of Rochester, is the newest member of JWV Kauffman Post #41.

Article about Alex in the Jewish leger from December 3, 1987.

157

Alex with myself and my sister Lillian in 1962 in Israel.

Alex's future wife Marie in 1946.

Ambassade de France
aux États-Unis

Washington, D. C. le   13 janvier 1992

François Mitterrand, Président de la République française

à

Mr. Alexander ROSENFELD

en hommage et en reconnaissance des services

rendus à la France

au cours de la guerre 1939-1945.

Pour le Président de la République
l'Attaché de Défense

*Certificate of recognition from the French President Francois
Mitterrand given to Alex for his actions rendered in France
in time of war, 1939 - 1945.*

NOTES

CHAPTER 1: EARLY BACKGROUND

1. Norman Davies, God's Playground, a History of Poland (NY: Columbia University Press) 378.
2. M.B. Biskupski, The History of Poland (CT: Greenwood Press) 85.
3. Ibid, 57.
4. Ibid, 85.
5. Jacob Apenszlak, Editor; Jacob Kenner, Dr. Isaac Lewin, Dr. Moses Polakiewicz, Co-Editors, The Black Book of Polish Jewry (NY: Howard Fertig) 256.
6. Norman Davies, God's Playground, a History of Poland (NY: Columbia University Press) 244.
7. Meltzer, A. Taking Root: Jewish Immigrants in America. Toronto: McGraw-Hill Ryerson, Ltd., 1976, 1
8. "Pinkas Hakehilot," Encyclopedia of Jewish Communities, 1984 ed., 278.
9. Celia Heller, On the Edge of Destruction, (NY: Schocken Books) 15-16.
10. Ibid.
11. Ibid., 14-17.
12. Ibid., 17.
13. M.B. Biskupski, The History of Poland (CT: Greenwood Press) 30.
14. Emmanuel Rigelblum, Polish-Jewish Relations During the Second World War (NY: Howard Fertig) 14-15.
15. Jacob Apenszlak, Editor; Jacob Kenner, Dr. Isaac Lewin, Dr. Moses Polakiewicz, Co-Editors, The Black Book of Polish Jewry (NY: Howard Fertig) 252.
16. Ibid., 254.
17. Ibid., 255.
18. "Pinkas Hakehilot," Encyclopedia of Jewish Communities, 1984 ed., 278.
19. "Cossacks" Compton's Encyclopedia 2000. CD-ROM. 1999.

CHAPTER 2: ALEX'S CHILDHOOD

1. Emmanuel Rigelblum, Polish-Jewish Relations During the Second World War (NY: Howard Fertig) 16.
2. Ibid., 11-14.
3. Jacob Apenszlak, Editor; Jacob Kenner, Dr. Isaac Lewin, Dr. Moses

Polakiewicz, Co-Editors, The Black Book of Polish Jewry (NY: Howard Fertig) 276-277.

4. Ibid., 276.

CHAPTER 3: ALEX'S BROTHER

1. "Pinkas Hakehilot," Encyclopedia of Jewish Communities, 1984 ed., 278-281.
2. Celia S. Heller, On The Edge of Destruction (NY: Schocken Books) 125,227.
3. "Pinkas Hakehilot," Encyclopedia of Jewish Communities, 1984 ed., 278-281.
4. Celia S. Heller, On The Edge of Destruction (NY: Schocken Books) 246.
5. Ibid. 246.
6. Emmanuel Rigelblum, Polish-Jewish Relations During the Second World War (NY: Howard Fertig) 11.
7. "Shtetl," My Jewish World, 1975 ed., 169-170.
8. "Germany-Dictatorship Under Hitler," Compton's Ency-clopedia, 2000.
9. M.B. Biskupski, The History of Poland (CT: Greenwood Press) 30.

CHAPTER 5: FLIGHT TO ST. GENOLE

1. Michael R. Marrus and Robert O. Paxton, Vichy France and the Jews (NY: Basic Books, Inc. Publishers) 65.
2. Maria Julia Cirurgiao and Michael D Hull, "Aristides de Sousa Mendes, Angel Against the Blitzkrieg," Lyons Network, Feb. 2001, <http://www.an-gelfire. com/tx/ filial/ mendes.html>.
3. Etta Shiber, in collaboration with Anne and Paul Dupre, Paris-Underground (NY: Charles Scribner's Sons) 22.
4. Maria Julia Cirurgiao and Michael D Hull, "Aristides de Sousa Mendes, Angel Against the Blitzkrieg," Lyons Network, Feb. 2001, <http://www.an-gelfire. com/tx/ filial/ mendes.html>.
5. "Europe Drifts Into World War II," Compton's Encyclopedia 2000, CD-ROM (Broderbund, 1999).
6. Edwin Quittenton, "Evacuation-The Diary of One Man's Experience," March 2000, <http://www.cyndislist.com/diaries.htm>.
7. "World War II and its Aftermath to 1952," <http://www.us-history.com/ chap_6.html>.
8. William Shirer, The Collapse of the Third Republic, (NY: Simon & Schuster) 438-439.
9. "World War II," The New Encyclopaedia Britannica, (Ency-clopaedia Britannica Inc., 1998).

10. M.B. Biskupski, The History of Poland (CT: Greenwood Press) 88.

11. "Maginot Line," The New Encyclopaedia Britannica, (Encyclopaedia Britannica, Inc., 1998).

CHAPTER 6: RETURN TO PARIS

1. "Fall of France,"(Compton's Encyclopedia 2000, CD-ROM (Broderbund, 1999).

2. "Vichy Government and Free French," Compton's Encyclopedia 2000, CD-ROM (Broderbund, 1999).

3. Etta Shiber, in collaboration with Anne and Paul Dupre, Paris-Underground (NY: Charles Scribner's Sons) 42.

4. Violette Wassem, "Violette's Story," July 1997, <http://www.timewitnesses. org/english>.

5. Jacques Adler, The Jews of Paris and the Final Solution (NY: Oxford University Press) 41.

6. Martin Gilbert, The Second World War (NY: Henry Holt & Co.) 129.

7. Michael Berenbaum, The World Must Know (NY: Little, Brown and Company) 68.

8. Jacques Adler, The Jews of Paris and the Final Solution (NY: Oxford University Press) 253.

9. Ibid., 9.

10. Ibid., 17

11. Don Lawson, The French Resistance (NY: Julian Messner) 33

12. Varian Fry, Assignment: Rescue, An Autobiography By Varian Fry (NY: Scholastic Inc.) 17,24,25,49.

CHAPTER 7: THE BLACK MARKET

1. VioletteWassem, "Violette's Story," July 1997, <http://www.timewitnesses. org/english>.

2. Michael R. Marrus and Robert O. Paxton, Vichy France and the Jews (NY: Basic Books, Inc., Publishers) 183-184.

3. Ibid., 223.

4. Jacques Adler, The Jews of Paris and the Final Solution (NY: Oxford University Press) p.11

5. Ibid., p.44.

6. Ibid., 224.

7. Jeremy Josephs, Swastika Over Paris (NY: Arcade Publishing) 103,106.

8. Ibid.

9. Jacques Adler, The Jews of Paris and the Final Solution (NY: Oxford University Press) 181.

10. Jeremy Josephs, Swastika Over Paris (NY: Arcade Publishing) 103.

CHAPTER 8: ASSIGNMENT AND RECEPTION OF WORK PAPERS

1. Alexander Van Gurp, "A Letter to Susan," 1983, <http:fox.nstn.ca/~avg/Susan.htm>.

2. Tom Bower, Klaus Barbie The Butcher of Lyons (NY: Pantheon Books) p55.

3. "Netherlands Slave Laborers," <http://fox.nstn.ca/~avg/indexenglish.htm>

4 "Holocaust Victim Assets Litigation," 9/11/2000, <http: www.nyed.uscourts.gov/pub/rulings/cv/1996/6974.99.pdf>.

5. Jacques Adler, The Jews of Paris and the Final Solution (NY: Oxford University Press) 42.

6. Ibid., 12.

7. Michael Berenbaum, The World Must Know (NY: Little, Brown and Company) 69.

8. M.B. Biskupski, The History of Poland (CT: Greenwood Press) 106.

9. Conrad Stein, World At War, Resistance Movements (Chicago: Childrens Press), 8-7.

10. Michael R. Marrus and Robert O. Paxton, Vichy France and the Jews (NY: Basic Books, Inc. Publishers) 185.

CHAPTER 10: THE FACTORY AT BREMENBURG

1. Alexander Van Gurp, "A Letter to Susan," 1983, <http: fox.nstn.ca/~avg/Susan. tm>.

2. Ibid.

3. Ibid.

CHAPTER 11: NEWS ABOUT STARY SONCZ

1. "Pinkas Hakehilot," Encyclopedia of Jewish Communities, 1984 ed., 278-281.

2. Ibid.

3. Lucy Dawidowicz, The War Against The Jews (NY: Holt, Rinehart & Winston) 117 and 203.

4. Ibid, 117.

5. "Pinkas Hakehilot," Encyclopedia of Jewish Communities, 1984 ed., 278-281.

6. Lucy Dawidowicz, The War Against The Jews (NY: Holt, Rinehart & Winston) 229.

7. "Pinkas Hakehilot," Encyclopedia of Jewish Communities, 1984 ed., 278-281.

8. Lucy Dawidowicz, The War Against The Jews (NY: Holt, Rinehart & Winston) 243.

9. "Pinkas Hakehilot," Encyclopedia of Jewish Communities, 1984 ed., 278-281.

10. Ibid.

11. Lucy Dawidowicz, The War Against The Jews (NY: Holt, Rinehart & Winston) 202.

12. "Pinkas Hakehilot," Encyclopedia of Jewish Communities, 1984 ed., 278-281.

13. Jacques Adler, The Jews of Paris and the Final Solution (NY: Oxford University Press) 187.

14. Ibid., 204.

15. Ibid., 45-46.

16. "Oskar Schindler," <http://teachwithmovies.org/guides/schindlers-list.html>.

17. Ibid.

18. Eric J. Greenberg, "In Pursuit of Justice," The Jewish Week, February 16, 2001.

19. Ibid.

CHAPTER 12: RELAXATION AND TRANSFERS

1. Violette Wassem, "Violette's Story," July 1997, <http://www.timewitnesses. org/english>.

2. Jacques Adler, The Jews of Paris and the Final Solution (NY: Oxford University Press) 32.

3. Jeremy Josephs, Swastika Over Paris (NY: Arcade Publishing) 59-73.

4. Jacques Adler, The Jews of Paris and the Final Solution (NY: Oxford University Press) 42-43

5. "The Righteous Among The Nations," France, <http://www.yad-vashem. org.il/righteous/bycountry/france/andre_trocme.html>.

6. Jacques Adler, The Jews of Paris and the Final Solution (NY: Oxford University Press) 45.

CHAPTER 13: MARIA

1. "Holocaust Victim Assets Litigation," 9/11/2000, <http:www.nyed.uscourts. gov/pub/rulings/cv/1996/6974.99.pdf>.

Chapter 14: Bombing Raids

1. "World War II," Compton's Encyclopedia 2000, CD-ROM (Broderbund, 1999).

Chapter 18: Escape To France

1. Jacques Adler, The Jews of Paris and the Final Solution (NY: Oxford University Press) 45.

Chapter 19: Journey to Azay Le Ferron

1. Conrad Stein, World At War, Resistance Movements (Chicago: Childrens Press) 21.

Chapter 20: Introduction to the French Underground

1. Tom Bower, Klaus Barbie The Butcher of Lyons (NY: Pantheon Books) 31-38.
2. Don Lawson, The French Resistance (NY: Julian Messner) 20-26.
3. Tom Bower, Klaus Barbie The Butcher of Lyons (NY: Pantheon Books) 31-38.
4. Conrad Stein, World At War, Resistance Movements (Chicago: Childrens Press) 20.
5. `Don Lawson, The French Resistance (NY: Julian Messner) 26-33.
6. `Jacques Adler, The Jews of Paris and the Final Solution (NY: Oxford University Press) 236.
7. `Ibid., 236.
8. `Conrad Stein, World At War, Resistance Movements (Chicago: Childrens Press) 31-43.
9. `Don Lawson, The French Resistance (NY: Julian Messner) 33.
10. Nathaniel Bornstein and Jessica Mendels, "29 Months in Exile," 1997 <http://www.29months.com/english/>.
11. Varian Fry, Assignment: Rescue, An Autobiography By Varian Fry(NY: Scholastic Inc.) 17,24,25,49.
12. Ibid., 3-4.
13. Ibid., 161.

Chapter 21: Underground Missions

1. "World War II," Compton's Encyclopedia 2000, CD-ROM (Broderbund, 1999).

Chapter 23: Return to Paris.

1. "World War II,"(Compton's Encyclopedia 2000, CD-ROM (Broderbund, 1999).

2. Etta Shiber, in collaboration with Anne and Paul Dupre, Paris-Underground (NY: Charles Scribner's Sons) 55.

3. Nathaniel Bornstein and Jessica Mendels, "29 Months in Exile," 1997 <http:// HYPERLINK "http://www.29months.com/english/" www.29months.com/english/>.

4. Cyril Black, Jonathan Helmreich, Paul Helmreich, Charles Issawi, and A. James McAdams, Rebirth, A History of Europe Since World War II (Colorado: Westview Press) 345.

5. Violette Wassem, "Violette's Story," July 1997, <http://www.timewitnesses.org/english>.

6. Ibid.

Chapter 24: Exodus to Israel

1. Museum of Tolerance Multimedia Learning Center, 4/4/01, HYPERLINK "http://motlc.wiesenthal.com/text/x01/xr0146.html" http://motlc.wiesethal.com/text/x01/xr0146.html

2. "How Israel Was Made," 3/18/01, HYPERLINK "http://home.talkcity.com/LibraryDr/zoozu/how2.htm" http://home.talkcity.com/LibraryDr/zoozu/how2.htm

3. Museum of Tolerance Multimedia Learning Center, 4/4/01,HYPERLINK "http://motlc, wiesenthal.com/text/x0146.html" http://motlc, wiesenthal.com/text/x0146.html

4. Ibid.

5. Ibid.

6. "Mers-El-Kebir,"<http://www.angelfire.com/ia/totalwar/MersElkebir.html>.

7. Museum of Tolerance Multimedia Learning Center, 4/4/01, HYPERLINK "http://motlc.wiesenthal.com/text/x01/xxr0146.html" http://motlc.wiesenthal.com/text/x01/xr0146.html

Epilogue

1. Marie Rosenfeld, Alex Rosenfeld's widow, interview.

Bibliography

Articles and Books

Adler, Jacques. The Jews Of Paris And The Final Solution. NY: Oxford University Press, 1987.

Apenszlak, Jacob, Editor; Kenner, Jacob; Lewin, Isaac, Dr.; Polakiewicz, Moses, Dr.; Co-Editors. The Black Book of Polish Jewry. NY: Howard Fertig, 1982.

Berenbaum, Michael. The World Must Know. NY: Little, Brown and Company, 1993.

Biskupski, M.B. The History of Poland. CT: Greenwood Press, 2000.

Black, Cyril; Helmreich, Jonathan; Helreich, Paul; Issawi, Charles; McAdams, A. James. Rebirth, A History of Europe Since World War II. Colorado: Westview Press, 1992.

Bower, Tom. Klaus Barbie, The Butcher of Lyons. NY: Pantheon Books, 1984.

Davies, Norman. God's Playground, A History Of Poland. NY: Columbia University Press, 1982.

Dawidowicz, Lucy. The War Against The Jews. NY: Holt, Rinehart & Winston, 1975.

Duboscq, Genevieve. My Longest Night. NY: Seaver Books, 1978.

Fry, Varian. Assignment: Rescue. NY: Scholastic Inc. 1968.

Gilbert, Martin. The Second World War. NY: Henry Holt & Co., 1989.

Greenberg, Eric J. "In Pursuit of Justice." The Jewish Week. February 16, 2001.

Heller, Celia. On the Edge of Destruction. NY: Schocken Books, 1977.

Josephs, Jeremy. Swastika Over Paris. NY: Arcade Publishing, 1989.

Lawson, Don. The French Resistance. NY: Julian Messner, 1984.

Marrus, Michael R. and Paxton, Robert O. Vichy France And The Jews. NY: Basic Books, Inc. Publishers, 1981.

Meltzer, A. Taking Root: Jewish Immigrants in America. Toronto: McGraw-Hill Ryerson, Ltd., 1976.

Rigelblum, Emmanuel. Polish-Jewish Relations During the Second World War. NY: Howard Fertig, 1976.

Shiber, Etta, in collaboration with Durpre, Anne and Paul. Paris Underground. NY: Charles Scribner's Sons, 1943.

Shirer, William. The Collapse Of The Third Republic. NY: Simon & Schuster, 1969.

Stein, Conrad. World At War, Resistance Movements. Chicago: Childrens Press, 1982.

ENCYCLOPEDIA

"Europe Drifts Into World War II." Compton's Encyclopedia 2000. CD-ROM. 1999.

"Fall Of France." Compton's Encyclopedia 2000. CD-ROM. 1999.

"Germany-Dictatorship Under Hitler." Compton's Encyclopedia 2000. CD-ROM. 1999.

"Jozef Pilsudski." Compton's Encyclopedia 2000. CD-ROM. 1999.

"Vichy Government and Free French." Compton's Encyclopedia 2000. CD-ROM. 1999.

"Maginot Line." The New Encyclopaedia Britannica. 1998.

"Pinkas hakehilot," Encyclopedia Of Jewish Communities. 1984. Vol. III.

"Shtetl." My Jewish World. 1975. Vol. V.

"Cossacks." Compton's Encyclopedia 2000. CD-ROM. 1999.

"World War II." The New Encyclopaedia Britannica. 1998.

INTERNET

Bornstein, Nathaniel and Mendels, Jessica. "29 Months in Exile." <http://www.29months.com/english/>.

Cirurgiao, Maria Julia; and Hull, Michael D. "Aristides De Sousa Mendes, Angel Against The Blitzkrieg." <http://www.angelfire.com/tx/filial/mendes.html>.

"Holocaust Victim Assets Litigation." <http:www.nyed.uscourts.gov/pub/rulings/cv/1996/697499.pdf>.

"How Israel Was Made."<http://home.talkcity.com/LibraryDr/zoozu/how2.htm>

"Learning Guide To Schindler's List."<http://teachwithmovies.org/guides/schindlers-list.html>.

"Mers-El-Kebir," <http://www.angelfire.com/ia/totalwar/MersElkebir.html>.

Museum Of Tolerance Multimedia Learning Center. "Deportation to Cyprus," "In Western Europe," "The Beginnings Of The Aliya Bet Movement," "The Heart of Zionist Activity," <http://motic.wiesenthal.com/text/xo1/xr0146.html>

"Netherlands Slave Laborers." <http://fox.nstn.ca/~avg?indexenglish.htm>. Quittenton, Edwin.

"Evacuation-The Diary Of One Man's Experience." <http://www.cyndislist.com/diaries.htm>.

Simon Wiesenthal Center Multimedia Learning Center Online. "Aliyah Bet." <http://motlc.wiesenthal.com/pages/t001.html>.

"The Righteous Among The Nations." France. <http://www.yad-vashem. org.il. / righteous/bycountry/france/andre_trocme.html>.

Van Gurp, Alexander. "A Letter To Susan."<http: www.nyed.uscourts.gov/pub/rulings/cv/1996/697499.pdf. >

Wassem, Violette. "Violette's Story." <http://www.timewitnesses.org/english>.

"World War II And Its Aftermath to 1952." <http://www.us-history.com/chap_6.html>.

OTHER

Central Intelligence Agency. Atlas of Eastern Europe. US Government Printing Office, 1990.

Rosenfeld, Marie. Alex Rosenfeld's widow. Interview. May 2001.

US Holocaust Memorial Museum. Historical Atlas of the Holocaust. NY: Simon and Schuster Macmillan, 1996.